THE SUNDAY TIMES

CREATING SUCCESS

Successful
Interviewing and Recruitment

Rob Yeung

KOGAN PAGE

This book is dedicated to the many Talentspace clients who have asked me to interview candidates on their behalf, train their interviewers, and design their assessment centres.

First Indian Edition 2009

Kogan Page India Private Limited
4737/23 Ansari Road,
Daryaganj
New Delhi 110 002

This edition is for sale in the Indian subcontinent only. Not for export elsewhere.

ISBN-10: 81-7554-465-1
ISBN-13: 978-81-7554-465-9

Published by Vinod Vasishtha for Kogan Page India Private Limited,
4737/23, Ansari Road, Daryaganj, New Delhi 110 002.

Printed and bound by Raj Press, R-3, Inderpuri, New Delhi - 110 012.

Contents

1

Why learn to interview properly?

It *almost* goes without saying that having the right employees is essential for building a strong team and a competitive organisation. But when it comes to interviewing candidates, no matter how good a judge of character you are, you could be better.

Most managers develop their own interview styles based on a combination of instinct and techniques picked up from when they themselves were interviewed. Bad interviewing practices get passed on from one generation of managers to the next.

It seems strange that managers are happy to devise and follow careful processes when it comes to handling financial, selling, customer service, disciplinary and most other business issues. But when it comes to hiring, most managers decide instead to follow the 'I'll know it when I see it' school of interviewing. However, research and practice shows that gut feelings are an incredibly unreliable way of identifying the best candidates. It is a proven fact that adopting a structured approach to interviewing is the best approach to separating most effectively the truly excellent candidates from the rest.

A good interview should have three main objectives:

1. to evaluate candidates in an accurate and fair manner in order to identify the candidate(s) who will add most value in the job;

2. to treat candidates in a professional and courteous manner so that they will want to work for your organisation;
3. to help candidates understand the nature of the job so they can decide whether they want to work for your organisation.

The rest of this chapter explains why the traditional, unstructured interview fails to meet these objectives and discusses how structured interviewing can help interviewers to get it right.

Interviewing is a skill

Most people think they are good judges of character and can discern how good other people are simply by having an informal conversation and asking them a few questions. However, the truth is that most people overestimate their ability to interview other people.

As a business psychologist, I have trained many managers and executives in interviewing skills, including partners in law firms and managing directors in investment banks. And even though these very senior people often run businesses that make tens of millions every year, I have to say that they are rarely naturally skilled interviewers. Asking the right questions to discern whom to hire is not a natural human talent. Unless people have been taught how to interview candidates, it is unlikely that they do so correctly.

Common misconceptions

Whenever I run a workshop to train managers in interviewing skills, I like to start by asking the participants how they can tell a good candidate from a bad candidate. Here are some of the comments I have heard:

- 'I can tell within the first minute whether a candidate's going to fit in or not.'

- 'You can tell from the way candidates shake hands whether they are right for the job.'
- 'A person with scuffed shoes is likely to be disorganised.'
- 'If someone doesn't look you in the eyes, you know he's hiding something.'
- 'Wearing a red tie is a sign of confidence.'
- 'Having worked this long in the business, I know a good candidate when I see one.'

Unfortunately, research tells us that interviewers who base their selection decisions on such preconceptions are likely to get it wrong as often as they are to get it right – they may as well just flip a coin to determine whom to hire.

What happens with many interviewers is that they get it right *some* of the time and simply remember those occasions when they got it right – they forget the times they got it wrong. Relying on gut feel, instinct, body language, or even appearance alone will *not* find you the best candidate.

Problems and errors

Interviewers fall prey to all sorts of problems and errors when it comes to trying to identify the candidate who will perform most strongly in the job:

- **Interviewers tend to rate more highly candidates that they *like*.** Interviewers tend to like (and therefore rate) candidates who have similar backgrounds, personality characteristics, or personal interests. Without consciously realising it, interviewers may ask easier questions of candidates they like and/or who are similar to themselves than the ones they don't like and/or who are dissimilar. It would be unfair for teachers at a school to set easier exams for the students they like than for those they don't – but that's precisely what many untrained interviewers do. The danger is that interviewers therefore 'clone' themselves, hiring people who play a similar sport or who studied similar subjects at school rather than other candidates who may be better for the job.

Of course you need to like the people who work for you, but most interviewers subconsciously rely too much on the likeability factor when it comes to hiring.

- **Many interviewers fall prey to the 'halo effect'.** They wrongly believe that a candidate who has charm and good interpersonal skills will be good at everything else. But the reality is that just because someone creates a good first impression during an interview does not mean that they will be good at other skills – even other interpersonal skills – such as working in a team or serving customers.
- **Interviewers are also prone to the 'horns effect',** allowing some minor negative aspect of the candidate to influence their impression of the candidate unduly. For example, a candidate arriving late and out of breath because their train was delayed (possibly due to no fault of their own) could get marked down disproportionately for having been late despite actually having quite good skills and experience.
- **Interviewers often rely too heavily on a strong CV and track record.** They assume that 'having the right background' of having worked in other, similar companies automatically means that the candidate must be good at the job. Interviewers may spend the duration of the interview simply having a chat to ensure that there's sufficient chemistry. But all that a good CV and track record shows is that a person delivered results for their previous company, with that company's own rules, ways of working, and people. That person could be a total flop when it comes to working for your organisation with different rules, ways of working, and people.

Reasons to get it right

The consequences of picking the wrong person could be costly or painful. You could end up with someone who is so bad that they annoy customers, make mistakes, lower morale amongst existing members of the team and lose your organisation money. You may end up having to spend more time managing, coaching and/or disciplining a new joiner or even having to go through the whole recruitment process again once the new joiner has quit or been fired.

The Chartered Institute of Personnel and Development estimated that the cost of hiring the wrong person is over £8,000 per employee. Given the high costs of getting it wrong, it pays to interview rigorously to get the best person in the job from the start.

Having a more diverse workforce

For years, it has been good enough for managers to hire people like themselves. However, research suggests that diverse teams may be more effective than homogenous ones (ie ones that are too similar). It shouldn't surprise you that having people in a team of a similar age, similar educational background, similar interests outside of work and so on could easily turn a team into a group of 'yes people', prone to agreeing with ideas that are generated within the team – even the bad ideas.

It's only when you have people with different backgrounds, experiences and perspectives that you get new ideas, constructive conflict and the best chance of tackling the broadest array of problems and situations. Effective interviewing allows you to find the best candidate, no matter how non-traditional their background.

Keeping on the right side of the law

Without clear criteria and a sound interviewing process, you could open yourself up to all sorts of legal troubles. Many interviewers say things like 'I'll know it when I see it', 'I'm looking for someone who fits into the team' or 'I need to find someone who has what it takes to succeed.' But if a candidate were to sue you for unfair discrimination, such explanations would not stand up in a court of law.

Fail to be able to explain exactly why you decided to take on one candidate over another and you could be in breach of employment law. The world is becoming increasingly litigious, with more and more candidates becoming aware of their options when it comes to suing organisations for unfair treatment during recruitment and selection. If your recruitment and selection interviews aren't demonstrably fair, it's probably only going to be a matter of time before you will get dragged into a court or tribunal by someone.

Creating a positive impression

Treating interview candidates poorly could give your organisation a bad reputation. The problem with informal, unstructured 'chat' interviews is that candidates may not feel that they were able to give a fair and full account of themselves. They may feel frustrated that they weren't given the chance to demonstrate properly their skills and abilities.

On the other hand, say you ask lots of hard-hitting questions in an aggressive manner to simulate some of the stress that they might expect on the job from colleagues or customers. If you do that, candidates may feel that you aren't treating them with enough consideration. Good candidates frequently have multiple options, and they could decide to accept a job offer from someone who treats them with a little more respect. Even worse, they may go bad-mouthing you and your business. Especially in an age in which many people write blogs and record their thoughts online, it's easy for even one or two angry candidates to give your organisation a bad reputation.

Good interviewers therefore leave candidates with a positive impression of the organisation by asking challenging (but appropriate) questions and behaving towards them with sufficient professionalism and respect. Think of it as good PR.

Two-way communication

Remember that part of the purpose of an interview is to help candidates decide whether they might want to work for your organisation. An effective interview should therefore also allow time for candidates to ask questions about the nature of the work, the people within the team, the reputation of the organisation, and any other issues they may want to talk about. The risk of not giving candidates a realistic preview of the job is that they might take up your job offer, discover that the job does not meet their expectations, and quit mere months or even weeks later.

2

Structuring the interview

Introducing the competency-based interview

Research from both top business schools and leading organisations tells us that a technique called *competency-based* interviewing is much more effective than unstructured interviewing at finding the person most suitable for the job. Also called *capability-based* or *behavioural* interviewing, the idea is to interview candidates against a set of criteria called competencies.

Competencies are simply: 'the skills, traits, qualities, and behaviours that contribute to effective performance in a job'. They are, effectively, what it takes for someone to be successful at work. Typical competencies may focus on skills such as problem solving, teamwork, leadership, communication, influence, customer service, and so on. The vast majority of large organisations, including consumer goods company Unilever, bank HSBC and retail giant Tesco, use competencies in their recruitment and selection processes. In a bid to increase their competitiveness, many smaller and medium-sized organisations are also adopting the competency-based approach.

By identifying and articulating the competencies that are necessary for each particular job, an interviewer can decide on appropriate questions to find the best person for the job. In order to make competency-based interviewing work, we need to follow two steps: know what you are looking for; ask the right questions.

Know what you are looking for

You must first have a clear idea of what a 'good' candidate looks like. If you don't know what you are looking for, the chances of finding it are slim. There's no point structuring an interview and asking certain questions unless you know what the answers should be.

Most untrained interviewers judge candidates on whether they match up to some implicit mental model of what 'good' looks like. The problem of judging candidates against an *implicit* mental model is that we can't tell if the mental models used by different interviewers are correct or even the same as each other's. It is only by making these mental models *explicit* – by talking about them with colleagues – that an organisation can check whether those assumptions of what 'good' looks like are correct. By agreeing with our colleagues about what it takes to perform well for any particular job, we can then make decisions that are based on the right characteristics rather than the wrong ones.

Your organisation needs two key documents. A *job description* is a list of the key tasks and responsibilities associated with a role; a *person specification* is a template of what the ideal candidate looks like.

If your organisation does not have these documents (or you need to update them), the rest of this chapter covers how to pull together a job description and a person specification in order to identify the competencies that will allow you to interview effectively.

Ask the right questions

Asking questions about teamworking may be inappropriate if you are recruiting a sales person who is going to spend all of their time visiting customers and no time at all working with colleagues. Or it may be less than useful to ask questions about a candidate's leadership skills if there is little opportunity for career progression in the vacancy you are trying to fill. Identifying the right competencies for the role is an important step. But the second step is to ask the right questions by using an appropriate interview structure.

In designing the structure for your interview, here are some broad principles to bear in mind as you read through the rest of the book:

1. **Ask only questions that are related to the job.** Always think about how each of your questions will help you to choose the best person for the job. A few minutes of chit-chat at the start of an interview may help to put a candidate at ease. However, the majority of your questioning should be about a candidate's relevant skills, experiences and motivations related to the job. Take care not to veer into conversation topics that are not related to the job, such as family matters, relationships outside of work, personal interests, and so on.
2. **Ask mainly questions that focus on past experience.** The key principle of competency-based interviewing is that *past behaviour is the most accurate predictor of future job success*. The vast bulk of the interview should be made up of questions, phrased in the past tense, that ask candidates about actual situations they have experienced.
3. **Aim for consistency.** An effective interview should also ask each candidate more or less the same questions in the same order to ensure that all candidates experience a consistent and fair process. Starting with a similar list of questions not only enhances consistency and effectiveness, but also makes interviewing easier for novice and/or nervous interviewers.

Remember, past behaviour is the single best predictor of future job performance. This is a fact that is supported by decades of research both by academics and by practitioners within a wide variety of organisations. I have already mentioned this fact and shall mention it again – but it is critically important as it forms the foundation for the whole concept of competency-based or behavioural interviewing.

The competency-based interview is quite different from the biographical style of interviewing that has been quite popular in the past. In a biographical interview, the interviewer takes a candidate through their CV, asking questions about their different jobs, their reasons for changing jobs, what they enjoyed or did not enjoy, and so on. However, research shows that asking such questions rarely allows interviewers to separate strong from weak candidates.

This kind of CV-based biographical interview is structured on what the candidate tells you on their CV. In contrast, the structure of a competency-based interview is based on what you, the interviewer, decide to ask the candidate, which makes it a much more powerful tool for you as an interviewer.

Pulling together a job description

There is no point conducting a structured competency-based interview that covers areas of skill that are not key to the role. The first step in preparing to run a competency-based interview is to prepare a job description, which then allows the drawing up of a person specification. The process of creating a job description is often called job analysis.

You can draw up a job description by talking to various experts across the organisation who are familiar with the requirements of the role. Or, as a minimum at least sit down for half an hour to write down what you believe are the requirements of the job. While you may be tempted to skip this step, it is essential to do some pre-interview preparation – not only in terms of finding the right person but also to be able to defend your selection decisions in a court of law.

A job description is also useful for advertising the role and helping potential applicants to decide whether to apply for the job. Once you have offered the job to a candidate, a job description can also help the eventual post-holder to understand what is required of them on a day-to-day basis.

A job description should include the following elements:

- job title;
- reporting relationships, including not only the job title of the supervisor or manager to whom the jobholder would be responsible but also the job titles of any employees who would report into the jobholder;
- summary of general nature and objectives of the job, which should usually be limited to a few sentences;
- list of main duties and responsibilities of the jobholder;
- terms and conditions of employment, which should include salary, holiday entitlement, benefits, and any other details such as whether the job is full time or part time, a permanent or temporary job, whether shift work is required, and so on.

Be careful in listing the duties or responsibilities. For example, a personal assistant or secretary may be considered to be responsible for the *accuracy* of the typing of a document, whereas his or her boss may have ultimate responsibility for the *content* of the document.

Table 2.1 Example job description for an assistant sales manager

Job title	Assistant sales manager.
Location	Richmond branch, London.
Reports	Reports into the branch sales manager. Four sales consultants report into the assistant sales manager role.
Objectives	To manage the team of sales consultants.
Duties	Distribute shop responsibilities to the sales consultants. Work to achieve customer satisfaction.

	Deal with customer complaints that are referred up by the sales consultants.
	Authorise customer refund requests.
	Place orders to replenish stock from head office.
	Work with the sales team to ensure the shop floor is clean and tidy at all times.
	Assist with other tasks as required by the store sales manager.
Terms	Basic salary plus 5 per cent sales commission. 35-hour week in shifts over the course of a 7-day week.

Table 2.2 outlines the job description for the role of a marketing director. As the role is more complex, the job specification is correspondingly more detailed.

Table 2.2 Example job description for a marketing director

Job title	Marketing Director UK
Location	Slough, UK
Reports	Reports to the UK Managing Director of XYZ Corporation. The Marketing Director has a team of 27 reports and four direct reports, which are: product marketing manager, customer marketing manager, sponsorship manager, customer insight manager.
Objective	Overall responsibility for promoting the XYZ brand in the UK while remaining consistent with XYZ's worldwide.
Duties	Responsible for market share, net revenues/profitability, and driving product to market. A marketing budget of £12 million. S/he will be accountable for: ■ Customer research, product development, and advertising activities. ■ Developing appropriate pricing policies. ■ Reviewing sales forecasts and working with sales to ensure achievement of sales and profit targets. ■ Reviewing staffing needs.
Terms	Salary to be agreed. Additional executive benefits including a stock option programme.

Creating a person specification

The next step in preparing to interview is to create a person specification, which is essentially a list of the human qualities needed to do the job. The person specification is an extension of the job description; while the job description outlines what the job entails, the person specification describes the kind of person who would be most suitable for the job.

The person specification outlines the minimum knowledge, experience, qualities and skills necessary to perform the job effectively. However, in preparing a person specification, it is important to note two important principles:

1. Qualities must be **job related.** Qualities that are not directly job related could result in unfair discrimination.
2. Qualities must be **realistic**. Having a very demanding set of requirements could be too restrictive and therefore result in too small a pool of candidates.

In relation to the first principle, for example, it might be nice to employ people who have similar hobbies and interests to you outside of work so that you have more in common with them. But that would not be job related and your organisation could therefore risk discriminating unfairly against candidates who might be able to do the job as well or even better, but who have different backgrounds from you and your existing colleagues.

In relation to the second principle, you might want to hire people with an MBA for all of the positions in your company, but is it realistic given the nature of the work and the salaries you are able to offer? As such, it is worth noting what is essential versus only desirable.

Typical headings

The section headings you use to write up a person specification matter less than the fact that you do write a person specification. Begin by looking at the job description and working out what the ideal jobholder would need to possess in order to do the job. Use the following headings as a guide:

- **Qualifications/training.** Are there any professional exams or technical qualifications that the jobholder must hold? While some jobs may require a particular qualification (eg a medical doctor), be careful not to stipulate particular qualifications if relevant experience may be just as good (eg for a software engineer, it may be that experience of using the software may be more important than merely having the right certificate or diploma).
- **Experience** of using a skill, eg supervising staff, managing budgets, conducting performance appraisals, negotiating with customers, and so on. Relevant experience may not always have come from doing paid work. A candidate may have experience of using a skill from their charity work, community groups, sporting pursuits, studies, and so on.
- **Knowledge and skills.** Think about the specific skills and knowledge that the jobholder must possess to handle the duties and responsibilities of the role successfully. These could include a working knowledge of software packages, fluency in particular languages, presentation skills, the ability to work under pressure, knowledge of employment law, and so on.
- **General/other attributes.** Include here any other qualities that you think are needed for the job, such as creativity, initiative, dependability, willingness to deal with repetitive work, ambition to achieve sales targets, self-confidence, and so on.

In creating your own person specifications, don't worry too much whether a quality you want to capture falls into one category or another. Just get it down on paper in a way that is useful to you.

Essential versus desirable requirements

Looking at the various requirements, consider whether each one is essential or merely desirable. For example, is it critical that someone is able to use a particular piece of software or would you be willing to train someone who has used similar software programs?

Setting minimum standards that are too high can leave you with too few candidates to choose from. With all of the above headings, be sure that you include only those qualities that are *both* job related *and essential* for the job. For example, many interviewers automatically assume that they want to hire people who are creative and possess initiative. But if you are looking to fill a vacancy that involves mainly repetitive work, people who are creative and possess initiative could easily get bored and decide to quit very quickly.

Table 2.3 is a person specification based on the example assistant sales manager job description (Table 2.1) above. As you can see, the person specification for this role is fairly simple. However, having captured the essential qualities necessary in the jobholder to be able to perform the job, you would now be ready to interview candidates.

Table 2.3 Example person specification for an assistant sales manager

Qualifications	None necessary.
Experience	At least 12 months' experience of supervising employees within a customer-facing environment, preferably in retail, is required. Two years essential, three or more years' experience of customer service desirable.
Skills	Customer service essential. Management skills essential. Communication skills essential. Computer literacy skills desirable. A working knowledge of the EGTM stock replenishment computer system would be desirable.
Other attributes	Enjoys working in a team. Takes the initiative when sales manager is not present. Neat and tidy physical appearance.

There is no single way to present the data within a person specification. Table 2.4 presents the person specification for a job as a public relations manager. As you can see, the information has been presented in a slightly different way. Choose whichever format makes most sense to you and your organisation.

Table 2.4 Example person specification for a public relations manager

	Essential	*Desirable*
Education	University degree (any subject)	PR or marketing-related degree
Experience	Understanding of PR and marketing Experience of writing for press	Experience of working in a press office or a PR consulting environment
Technical skills/knowledge	High level of proficiency in word-processing packages	Experience of desktop publishing software
General skills	Writes accurate and engaging copy for a range of audiences	Structures and delivers simple presentations to colleagues and clients

Creating job documents for your organisation

If you need to create a job description and/or a person specification for a role, the best way to do so is by talking to key stakeholders or people who are familiar with the role. Try to get time with: current incumbents who hold the role; supervisors or managers who would be in charge of the people that you are looking to recruit; people who previously held the role.

In your discussions with these stakeholders, you need to gather views as to:

- the goals and objectives of the role;
- the tasks the person in the role would be expected to perform as well as the results they would be expected to achieve;
- their responsibilities; the knowledge, skills and other personal characteristics that the successful candidate would need in order to do the job well;
- any qualifications and/or level of education that would be required for the role.

In asking these questions of stakeholders, think about both current and likely near-future goals, objectives and responsibilities. If you know that the nature of the role may need to change in the next few months, think about what skills, attributes or other qualities may be needed to meet those future demands.

Bear in mind also that some responsibilities may need to be performed frequently (eg opening and closing up a shop on a daily basis), while other responsibilities may only be intermittent (eg performing a monthly stock take or preparing for a quarterly sale event). Still other responsibilities may be performed only during emergencies (eg being responsible for first aid during a fire emergency). So make sure you prompt stakeholders by asking about frequent, intermittent and emergency activities to ensure you do not miss any important responsibilities or duties.

However, remember that while stakeholders may talk about qualities and attributes that they would like to see in the *ideal* candidate, you should always try to establish what is *necessary and realistic*. Consider some of these questions to challenge the thinking of stakeholders: 'Why couldn't someone without those skills and knowledge perform the main duties and responsibilities of the job?' 'Is that a necessary requirement for someone to be able to do the job – or is it merely a nice-to-have?'

Updating pre-existing written documents

Even if your organisation already has a job description and a person specification, it is worth checking that they are still up to date. The pace of the working world is such that much can have changed in as little as a year.

Has the job changed since the job description was last updated? Have changes in the composition of the team, shifting demands from other departments, the introduction of new technology or evolving customer needs altered the skills, knowledge or other attributes required of the ideal candidate? Talk to colleagues within the team if you are unsure.

3

Developing your questioning skills

As the interviewer, it is up to you to ask the right questions to find out whether the candidate has the skills and experience to fill the role. How your questions are constructed will determine the sorts of response you are likely to receive. Candidates will follow your lead, so if you ask poorly phrased questions they will give you information that hinders rather than helps you to find out whether they could do the job. This chapter covers the different types of questions that you may need to use throughout the interview to steer the candidate into telling you what you want to know.

While this chapter covers the broad questioning styles that you will need to use, we will come to cover exactly what questions you should ask in Chapter 8.

Asking open and closed questions

As an interviewer, your aim is to get the candidate talking for the bulk of the interview. As a rule of thumb, aim to get candidates talking for around 80 per cent of the time. You can achieve this by asking open, as opposed to closed, questions.

Closed questions

Closed questions are questions in which you could reasonably expect an answer of either a single word or a short phrase. Such questions are often used to confirm factual information or to elicit a simple 'yes' or 'no' response. Examples include:

- 'You were promoted to a supervisory role two years ago, weren't you?'
- 'When did you leave that last job?'
- 'How long is your notice period?'
- 'What newspaper do you read?'

Closed questions can serve several purposes:

- They allow you to get at simple facts (eg when you wish to probe for specific details).
- They are straightforward to answer and can be a way to get nervous candidates used to answering some simple questions to help them relax at the start of the interview.
- They allow you, the interviewer, to retain control of the conversation (eg if you find that a candidate is talking too much).

Closed questions hardly allow a candidate to speak other than to confirm basic facts about themselves. As such, you should use them only occasionally during the interview, eg at the start of the interview to check any grades achieved at school or dates of employment that may have been omitted on a CV or application form.

Open questions

In order to hear about candidates' experiences and get to evaluate whether they have the skills you need to fill the vacancy, you need to ask open questions that make it difficult for candidates to answer in a monosyllabic 'yes' or 'no' fashion.

Open questions are questions to which there are many possible answers, for example:

- 'What made you decide to enter this profession?'
- 'Tell me about a time you felt angry at work.'
- 'How much do you know about our organisation?'
- 'Why do you read the newspaper you read?'

Open questions have the following characteristics:

- They allow candidates to reflect and comment on their experiences, opinions or feelings.
- They invite the candidate to give lengthier responses.
- They cede control of the conversation to the candidate.

In preparing the questions you wish to ask during the interview, aim to ask a greater number of open questions rather than closed questions.

Asking reflective questions

An interview is about asking probing questions to understand a candidate's behaviour and motivations. However, there is a fine line to be drawn between asking sufficiently penetrating questions and asking so many questions that the candidate feels as if he or she is being interrogated.

Reflective remarks or questions attempt to paraphrase back to the candidate what you believe you have heard. They can serve several purposes:

- They can help you to check that you have understood correctly what a candidate has been telling you. Particularly when a candidate has given you a lengthy and rambling story, you can paraphrase or use a reflective question to summarise what you think you heard. The candidate can then confirm or disconfirm your understanding.

- They can help to put a candidate at ease, eg by showing that you empathise with a difficult situation that they experienced.
- They help to demonstrate to the candidate that you are listening attentively to what is being said.

Examples of reflective remarks and questions include:

- 'So you ended up having to work over the weekend to meet the customer's request?'
- 'Would I be right then to say that you enjoy having a fairly predictable routine at work?'
- 'It sounds as if you enjoy the financial aspects of the job more than the people side.'
- 'So it affects you very personally when people criticise your performance.'

Other reflective questions and statements could begin with phrases such as:

- 'If I understand you correctly, you…'
- 'So would it be true to say that you…'
- 'In other words, what you did was to…'

Reflective questions can be a good way to recap or finish off your discussion about one skill or area of a candidate's experience before moving on to another one.

Asking challenging questions

Candidates sometimes talk in universal terms about themselves or the situations they have been in. For example, they may make statements such as:

- 'I *never* make any mistakes.'
- 'I *always* leave my clients completely satisfied.'

- '*None* of my projects has ever gone over budget.'
- '*All* of my colleagues think I'm a good leader.'
- '*Everyone* thought that it was a bad idea.'

When candidates make such universally broad statements, you may wish to challenge their point of view. For example, candidates do sometimes exaggerate their own importance. Or they may underestimate the nature of a problem. When you wish to challenge the candidate's point of view, think about asking questions such as:

- '*Never*? Can you not think of even the smallest mistake or error you've made in the last 12 to 18 months?'
- 'You say that you *always* leave your clients satisfied. Who amongst your clients has been the least satisfied?'
- '*None*? Which of your projects was the closest to running over budget?'
- 'You say that *all* of your colleagues think you're a good leader? How do you know that for a fact?'
- 'Absolutely *everyone*? Did no one have any doubts?'

Challenge questions are by their nature provocative – they are intended to stop candidates in their tracks and make them rethink their point of view. However, be careful to pay close attention to your tone of voice and body language. Given the nature of these questions, it is quite easy to slip into coming across as disbelieving or aggressive.

Learning to ask questions about competencies and behaviour

We established in Chapter 2 that a key principle of structured, competency-based interviewing is to ask mainly questions that focus on past experience, ie to ask questions about actual, specific situations that the candidate has experienced in the past. This is because the best predictor of future behaviour is past performance.

During the interview, think of yourself as a detective collecting *evidence* about candidates' strengths and weaknesses. By asking candidates to talk about specific situations (and discussing them in quite a lot of detail), you can look for patterns of behaviour and also understand the extent to which candidates possess the skills you are looking for.

In order to guide candidates and make sure they give you actual examples of specific situations, you may need to be quite specific about the way in which you ask your questions too. As such, your questions will often sound more like instructions than traditional questions. For example, consider the following:

- 'Tell me about a time you managed a project.'
- 'Please give me an example of a situation in which you exceeded a customer's expectations.'
- 'Talk me through a difficult decision you had to make.'
- 'Tell me about a time you persuaded someone to change their mind.'

Remember, the key to asking effective behavioural questions is to make sure you ask questions that are phrased in the *past tense* and expect answers that are phrased in the past tense too. You will find that candidates commonly slip back into the present tense, for example answering 'I generally try to…' or 'My approach is to…' In my experience, I have observed that while interviewers usually find the notion of asking about past behaviour straightforward enough, they frequently struggle to ensure that candidates stick to talking about real situations.

Good opening questions that focus on past behaviour will typically begin with phrases such as:

- 'Tell me about a time…'
- 'Give me an example of a situation in which you…'
- 'Talk us through an instance when you…'
- 'Describe a situation in which you needed to…'

Notice that these questions allow candidates to pick whatever examples they feel are most appropriate. This is especially important for graduates and school leavers who may have little or no work experience. For candidates applying for entry-level positions, asking open-ended questions can allow them to talk about relevant examples from either their studies or activities they do in their spare time such as having participated in sports teams, organised church fetes, contributed to local community groups, and so on. Even for candidates who have more work experience, allowing candidates to select experiences from outside of their work may allow them to talk about hidden talents that they do not currently get to demonstrate in their paid work.

The funnelling technique

Asking a good opening question should be only the start of your questioning about how a candidate handled a particular situation. Candidates rarely share enough (or the right) information to allow you to judge their level of skill in handling different situations; you will need to ask further questions to understand exactly how candidates handled the situations they were in.

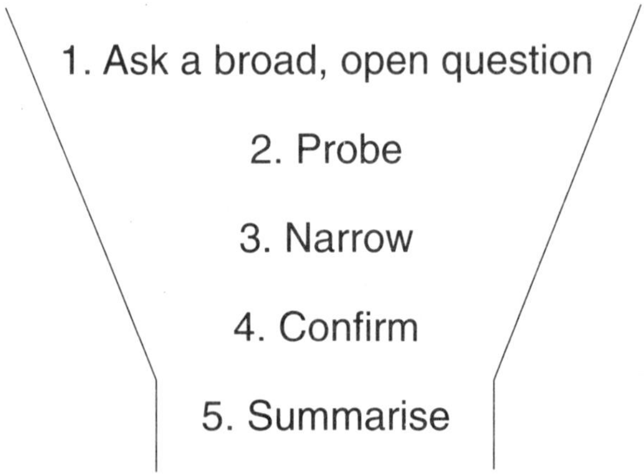

Figure 3.1 The funnelling technique

Figure 3.1 outlines the *funnelling technique*, which will allow you to probe candidates' responses in greater depth. The idea of this technique is to begin with a fairly broad question, allowing the candidate to pick whatever example they feel is most appropriate. As you ask further questions, the discussion becomes more and more specific – until it narrows down onto specifics of exactly what happened and the outcomes that were achieved.

The STARS technique

An easier to remember way of looking at the funnelling technique is to use the STARS acronym, as illustrated in Figure 3.2. Taking each of the STARS steps in turn:

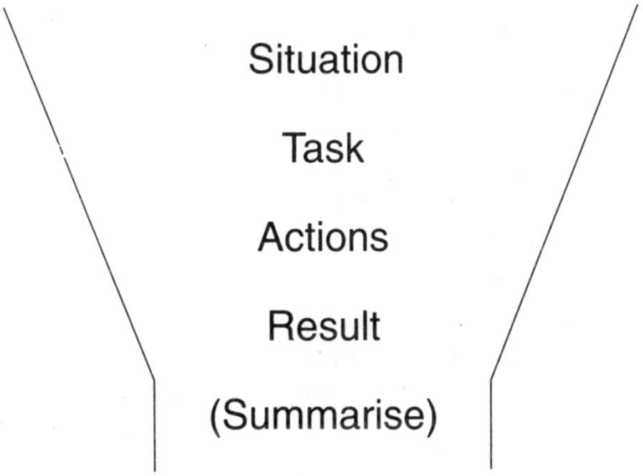

Figure 3.2 The STARS technique

1. **Situation.** Begin by asking a broad, open question about a *specific example of past behaviour*. These questions should typically begin with phrases such as 'Tell me about a time when you...' or 'Give us an example of a situation in which you...'
2. **Task.** Ask a question about the candidate's specific role in the situation. Quite often, the situation may have involved

many people, so ask questions such as: 'What was your role in this example?' or 'So what were *you* required to do in this situation?'
3. **Actions.** Possibly the most important part, try to understand the specific actions the candidate took to address the situation. Consider questions such as: 'What did you say or do?' 'What steps did you take to tackle the opportunity/rectify the problem?'
4. **Result.** Finish off by asking what result the candidate achieved in the end. If appropriate, you may also wish to ask questions about what lessons the candidate learnt.

If you are in any doubt as to what you heard, a fifth step may be to summarise in a few sentences what you think the candidate told you. By reflecting back what you think you heard, you can check that you understood the situation correctly.

Consider a couple of worked examples. Say you are trying to understand a candidate's ability to prioritise their workload. The questions might look as shown in Table 3.1.

One reason for asking 'when' the situation happened is to check whether it happened relatively recently or a long time ago. For example, if a candidate says that the situation occurred five or six years ago, you may wish to ask for a more recent example that he or she should be able to remember more accurately. If the candidate finds it difficult to come up with a more recent example, that in itself could tell you that the skill you are probing is not one that the candidate exercises much. Remember also that all of your questions should be phrased in the past tense.

Consider the questions in this example as a *suggestion* as to questions you may need to ask. Obviously, if the candidate tells you about some piece of information without needing to be prompted, you may not need to ask some of your questions.

The precise questions (and the order of those questions) matter less than the fact that you probe in sufficient detail to understand exactly what happened, how the candidate responded, why the candidate chose to behave that way, and how the situation turned out in the end.

Table 3.1 Sample STARS funnel

1. **Situation**	'Describe an occasion when you planned and organised a difficult project.' 'When did this happen? How long ago was this?'
2. **Task**	'What exactly were you trying to achieve?' 'What problems or difficulties did you encounter?'
3. **Actions**	'How did you tackle that first problem?' 'How did you tackle that second problem?' 'How did you deal with that final problem?'
4. **Result**	'What was the outcome of it all?'
5. **Summarise (if necessary)**	'So you...'

Focusing in on actions

It is pointless asking broad, open questions without following them up with probing questions about the specific actions that the candidate took to deal with the situation. In fact, *the most important questions to ask are around the actions that the candidate took*. Within the STARS acronym, consider the 'A' the most critical letter.

Candidates usually choose to talk about situations that turned out well. But what you must find out is the extent to which the candidate was responsible for that success – was it down to the candidate or to other factors such as the hard work of other members in the team or even just plain luck?

If candidates talk in overly broad terms about what they did, make sure you ask further questions such as:

- 'That's quite a broad statement, please tell me exactly what you did.'

- 'Take me through how you did that, one step at a time.'
- 'Go back to the beginning for me when you figured out there was a problem and tell me exactly how you started to deal with it.'
- 'What exactly did you do next?'
- 'And what was your next step?'

Notice that these questions can be asked with a question mark (eg 'How exactly did you deal with the angry supplier?') or without a question mark and phrased instead as a statement (eg 'Tell me exactly what you did to deal with the angry supplier'). Generally speaking, asking questions rather than making statements is preferred, as the latter can – if asked in the wrong tone of voice – be misinterpreted as more forceful.

Candidates are rarely used to talking in specific detail about exactly what they did in a situation. For example, in answer to the question 'How did you decide that?' a candidate may well respond 'We had a discussion about it.' A good interviewer should then ask: 'When you say "we had a discussion about it", what *exactly* did *you* do or say in that discussion?'

By asking further questions, you are aiming to be able to describe what the candidate said and did and thought as if you had been a 'fly on the wall' during the situation. In asking questions about any particular competency, do not be surprised if you need to ask questions about the candidate's actions at least several or even half-a-dozen times. Consider also the following suggestions for probing further into a candidate's actions:

- 'How did you achieve that exactly?'
- 'What other options did you consider before taking that course of action?'
- 'What did the customer/your boss/your colleague/the supplier/etc say next?'
- 'How did you respond to that?'
- 'What exactly did you do next?'
- 'Tell me more about your meeting with that person and what you did.'

One particularly useful technique is to paraphrase back what the candidate has told you before asking for more specific detail about what he or she did. In general terms, you might ask: 'You say that you [action taken by candidate]. How did you do that exactly?' or 'You said earlier that you [action taken by candidate]. Precisely what did you do or say?' Consider these examples:

- 'You say that you pacified the customer. How did you do that exactly?'
- 'You say that you sold a lot more that year. Can you remember how many exactly?'
- 'You mentioned earlier that you disciplined the member of staff. What exactly did you do or say?'
- 'So you're saying that you reduced absenteeism. Talk me through step-by-step precisely what you did to achieve that.'
- 'In creating your spreadsheet, tell me about the data sources you used in it and how you put it together.'
- 'You say that you resolved the situation. Could you explain how you did that?'

As you can see, many of these probing questions relate specifically to what the candidate has said. As such, it is difficult to prepare a totally comprehensive list of probing questions in advance of an interview. While you may be able to prepare some probing questions, part of becoming a skilled interviewer is learning to think on your feet to come up with further, relevant questions to ask about candidates' actions. At the same time, you should skip questions that you may have prepared ahead of time for which you have already received answers.

Remember, after asking a question about a situation that a candidate has been in, you should focus in particular on their *actions* to understand exactly what they were doing and thinking at the time.

Quantifying results

Candidates sometimes also talk in vague terms, by using comparators such as 'better', 'worse', 'less', 'more' and so on. In order to understand exactly the results that a candidate claims to have achieved, you may wish to ask questions such as:

- 'Could you quantify that for me please?'
- 'You say "better". Compared to what?'
- 'You mentioned that you have fewer problems. How many exactly?'

Separating 'I' from 'we'

When talking about the nature of their actions, another common situation is for a candidate to talk continually in the plural – 'we made a decision to…', 'the team and I agreed not to…', etc. When a candidate talks about what 'we' (ie the team) did, you should try to separate out the candidate's role from that of his or her colleagues. Try questions such as: 'You say "we". Who else was involved? What was *your* contribution?' 'You say that the whole team was involved in that. Could you explain what *your* specific role in that was, please?'

Understanding the candidate's thinking

It's not always enough simply to know *how* a candidate behaved in different situations. A good interviewer may need occasionally to understand *why* the candidate chose to behave that way. Otherwise, it could just be possible that a candidate demonstrated the right behaviours by random chance rather than through their forethought and insight!

Try occasionally to ask not only *what* the candidate did, but also *why* they chose to do it that way, with questions such as:

- 'Why did you do it that way?'
- 'What were you thinking at that point?'

- 'What other options did you consider at the time?'
- 'What would the consequences have been of not doing that?'
- 'At the time, what did you think the pros and cons of doing that were?'

Asking for further examples

To investigate a candidate's performance with regard to each competency, *you should aim to ask (at least) two broad, open questions per competency* (see Chapter 8 for examples of different questions that you could use). Asking for two examples allows you to collect more evidence than if you ask only one question. You are better off probing a smaller number of competencies in detail than gathering superficial evidence about a larger number of competencies.

Seeking contrary evidence

Competency-based interviewing is not only about looking for evidence that candidates have in the past demonstrated the behaviours you are looking for. You should also use it as an opportunity to explore the areas in which candidates struggle. For example, if the job requires customer service skills, you would naturally ask questions about situations in which candidates successfully dealt with customers' needs. However, you may gather more useful information by asking the opposite question: 'Tell me about a different time when you failed to meet a customer's needs.' Or if you were asking candidates to tell you about an occasion on which they successfully coached someone, try asking the opposite question about an occasion on which they coached someone but did not achieve a satisfactory outcome.

By asking questions about failures as well as successes, you will get not only a picture of what candidates do well but also what they don't do so well.

A worked example

To give you an idea of what one competency-based interview funnel might look like, consider the following an example exchange between an interviewer (I) and a candidate (C):

I: 'Can you give me an example of a project that you're particularly proud of having managed?'

C: 'I suppose my style of managing projects is to plan things from the beginning and then drive them to completion. I try to —'

I: (Interrupts candidate, as the candidate is talking in general terms about herself rather than about a single example) 'Sorry, but do you have a *specific* example of a project you've managed that you could talk about, please?'

C: 'OK. I was asked to organise a party for our clients. We have about three or four parties a year for clients and we use them as opportunities to sell them some of our other services. My boss asked me to organise a party. So I chose a theme, liaised with the venue, dealt with caterers, and on the day made sure everyone was happy.'

I: 'When did this happen?' (Checking that the example is recent and therefore a good example of the candidate's skill)

C: 'This must have been last summer, so probably 9 months ago.'

I: 'I'd like to take you back to the beginning and get you to talk me through exactly how you organised the party. When your boss asked you to take on the responsibility, what instructions did he or she give you?' (Asking the question to try to understand the task that the candidate took on. Was she an integral part of organising the party?)

C: 'Well, I'd organised the previous party before that, so his instructions were to do pretty much the same. I've organised a few client parties now so what I generally do is —'

I: (Interrupts again as candidate is once more talking in general terms rather than about the specific situation) 'Just going back to this particular occasion, how many people was the party to be for?'

C: 'We invited around 350 clients.'

I: 'And what budget were you given?'

C: 'Actually there is no set budget. One of the things we had to do was to put together a plan to show to my boss for signing off.'

I: 'You say "we" had to put together a plan. Who else was involved and what was your role?' (Asking the question to understand the candidate's specific contribution to the task)

C: 'Oh, sorry. I talked the party through with some of my colleagues to get ideas. But at the end of the day, I was solely responsible for the project. So it was up to me to put together a convincing case. In this instance, I researched a number of different venues and put together the costings and wrote a proposal explaining why I thought we should go with a garden party at a five-star hotel just outside the city.'

I: 'When you say you researched different options, what did you do precisely?' (Again, asking this question to understand the candidate's precise actions – did she have an integral role or was she only helping someone else?)

C: 'I have lots of contacts within the conference-organising field, so I called them and e-mailed them for suggestions. Plus I looked on the internet for ideas. And I keep a folder of ideas for future venues, so I looked through that as well. And of course I told the other people within my team and asked them for ideas too.'

I: 'So what did you propose to your boss in the end?' (Another question about actions)

C: 'We'd had some feedback from the previous client party that a lot of people had had difficulty finding parking. So this time having a venue that could take several hundred cars was a real priority. Plus because you can never count on the weather, I wanted to find a venue where either there was some indoor space or we could put up a marquee. We also needed to find somewhere that was not just a conventional, boring old hotel – as we wanted it to feel special and make it worth our clients taking a Saturday afternoon away from whatever else they could be doing to spend the day with us.'

I: 'So what were the most significant problems you encountered along the way?' (Finding out more about the candidate in this example)

C: 'The biggest panic was about three weeks beforehand when I tried calling the caterer and after a couple of attempts to get through found out that they'd gone out of business. So I spent a frantic couple of days phoning round other catering firms and setting up meetings to discuss menu plans and options and, of course, costs. But in the end I did find a firm that could cater the event and in fact they provided with us a slightly better menu at the same price.'

I: 'And what feedback did you get from your clients and boss after the event?' (Confirming the result of the project)

C: 'We had over three-quarters of the people we'd invited turn up, which was better than the usual 60 or 65 per cent of people who turn up. And my boss told me that the sales team picked up some new sales leads, which is precisely what the party was supposed to do.'

I: 'Thank you. Can we move on to another area. I'd like to ask...'

As you can see, the interviewer is constantly asking questions to keep the candidate talking about a *single* example and asking further questions to get at the *specific* actions that the candidate took in organising the event. Most experienced interviewers trained in the competency-based interviewing technique find that they have to ask a question approximately every minute or two – and often even more.

Catching liars out

As you can see, the competency-based interviewing style asks candidates to talk about what they did in a lot of detail. As such, competency-based interviewing happens to be a good way to catch out candidates who may be exaggerating, embellishing, or telling outright lies about their skills.

For example, say a candidate claims to have worked as part of a successful team that solved a lot of problems for their employer. By asking questions as to *exactly* what the candidate's contribution was, what decisions were made and exactly why they were made, and so on, you might very well discover that the candidate was only responsible for taking notes during meetings and little else!

If a candidate has told a story that is anything apart from wholly honest, the response will not hold up during the barrage of probing questions that you ask. So while the initial question phrased in the past tense is important, it is actually the quality of the follow-up questions that is more critical.

Delving into motivations and aspirations

Questions about a candidate's past behaviour in real situations should form the bulk of the interview. However, in deciding whom to hire, you may also wish to spend a part of the interview considering a candidate's level of motivation and their career aspirations.

For example, candidates who are more motivated will typically have done more research to understand the nature of the job. Candidates who have taken the time to find out about the minuses as well as the pluses of the job are likely to be more committed to the job.

As another example, think about the match between a candidate's personal aspirations and what your organisation is able to offer in terms of promotion. For example, say an organisation is looking to hire candidates, but that the organisation is growing only very slowly and therefore has only extremely limited opportunities to promote people. If that's the case, the organisation may not want to hire someone who is very driven, thrusting and ambitious. On the other hand, consider a different organisation that is growing aggressively and needs people who want to move into management. There may be little point hiring someone who only enjoys being a follower and has no aspirations of ever becoming a leader.

In order to explore candidates' motivations and aspirations, you may wish to ask questions such as:

- 'Why do you want to enter this profession?'
- 'What do you think you will be doing on a day-to-day basis?'
- 'What do you think you might be doing in an average week?'
- 'What do you know about the downsides of this profession?'
- 'What are your future career aspirations?'
- 'How do you see this role fitting into your overall career development?'

In asking such questions, there are no right or wrong answers. Answers to competency-based questions can be evaluated as good or bad. But the answers to questions about candidates' motivations and aspirations depend on the nature of the role, the prospects for promotion and growth for the successful candidate, and the culture of your organisation.

Interpreting body language

The topic of understanding human body language could fill a book in itself. A book such as this on recruitment and selection interviewing simply can't cover the topic in enough detail.

It is in fact dangerous to read too much into a candidate's body language. For example, a candidate who crosses their legs during an interview may simply have learnt in their upbringing that it is polite to do so when meeting strangers. Or they may cross their legs simply because it is a comfortable way to sit. Crossed legs do not always signify defensiveness!

Similarly, fidgeting or the avoidance of eye contact could both be interpreted in several ways. Some people think that they signify lying. But they could just as readily indicate that the candidate is nervous – perhaps because he or she desperately wants this job and is simply very aware of what is at stake.

It may be more useful to use a candidate's body language and tone of voice as another point of discussion. In particular, look out for changes in their body language. If someone fidgets more or sounds distressed or excited, then mention it and see how the candidate responds.

The best thing to do is try to discuss what you think you see by using reflective statements or questions such as:

- 'You seem quite nervous – how do you feel at the moment?'
- 'I get the impression that you find too many customer phone calls quite irritating.'
- 'Watching you come to life telling me about that situation, I get the feeling that you get the biggest buzz from working under pressure.'

By broaching the subject, you allow the candidate to explain their emotional reaction to you rather than you making assumptions that may be incorrect.

Being persistent

Say you ask a candidate: 'Tell me about a time when you dealt with a difficult colleague.' The candidate may scratch their head and say that they can't think of an example. However, do not simply move on to the next question. If a question was worth asking in the first place, you should persist. Candidates should not be allowed to avoid answering questions simply because they find them difficult.

When asked to share with you examples of specific situations, a few candidates may not be able to give you an answer immediately. Perhaps they feel nervous and simply cannot bring to mind a relevant example. If this happens, try some of the following techniques to try to draw a relevant example from the candidate:

- Say to the candidate that it's OK to spend some time thinking about an example. Give the candidate up to perhaps a minute – or even more if time allows – to reflect on their experience. Given a little bit of time, many candidates will be able to come up with a relevant example.
- Ask the question in a different way. Rephrase the question for the candidate using slightly different words. For example, if you have already asked a question such as 'Tell me about a difficult customer that you dealt with', try alternatives such as 'When was the last time a customer made you feel angry? Tell me about it' or 'Tell me about a recent occasion a customer made life difficult for you.'
- Ask a completely different question relating to the same skill area. For example, say you are testing a candidate's ability to work in a team and have already asked 'Tell me about a team you were proud to be a part of and explain your role.' You could ask different questions about teamworking such as 'Tell me about an occasion when you helped out a teammate' or 'Give me an example of a time a teammate asked you for help.'
- Move on to a different topic, but make a note to return to the same area of questioning later during the interview.

Even after several attempts to ask the question in different ways or at a later point during the interview, it is possible that a candidate may still struggle to come up with an example. If you have exhausted all of the means at your disposal to investigate a candidate's skill in a particular area, you should take their lack of response as a lack of evidence that they possess skill in that area. Perhaps the candidate cannot come up with an example because he or she has never exercised that skill. To put it another way, a lack of response is likely to indicate that he or she does not have one of the skills you need for the job.

4

Avoiding poor questions

The most difficult part of learning to use a competency-based interview structure is not so much to do with learning what questions to ask; the greater difficulty is often in learning what questions to *avoid* asking. There are some questions that are illegal because they discriminate unfairly against certain candidates. However, there are also many other questions that *should* not be asked simply because they are ineffective questions.

Some interviewers ask interview questions that they have heard being used by other interviewers; many interviewers use questions that they have themselves been asked in the past. But just because a question has been used by another interviewer does not automatically make it an effective question. On the surface, many of the questions contained within this chapter may appear to be the questions that clever interviewers might wish to ask. But in reality, these questions rarely help you to gather information that will allow you to make the right selection decision.

Unacceptable and discriminatory questions

An interview is obviously a tool used to discriminate (ie distinguish or tell the difference) between strong and weak candidates. However, as interviewers in the past have used the interview to discriminate *unfairly* against people for inappropriate reasons, there are now certain interview questions that should be avoided.

It is now illegal to discriminate against candidates based on race or ethnicity, nationality or ancestry, religious beliefs, gender, age, sexual orientation, marital status, disability status, political beliefs, union affiliation, and many topics to do with candidates' personal lives such as whether they have children or with whom they reside. While it seems that this is a long list of topics that you are not allowed to ask about, the principle is actually quite simple: *Focus only on asking questions that are directly related to the job.*

Speaking from a technical point of view, there are no questions that are 'legal' or 'illegal'. For example, asking a candidate 'Are you married?' is not in itself a prosecutable offence. However, asking the question could be taken as evidence of discriminating unfairly against a candidate based on marital status. As such, certain questions are unacceptable or discriminatory rather than being strictly illegal. Irrespective of whether questions are strictly speaking 'illegal' or merely 'unacceptable', organisations that allow interviewers to ask unacceptable questions run the risk not only of being exposed to costly legal penalties but also of causing offence to candidates that could result in a poor reputation for the organisation.

Before we get into the detail of the questions that you can and cannot ask, try working your way through a quiz. Go through the questions in Table 4.1 and tick the appropriate 'yes' or 'no' boxes before reading on.

Table 4.1 Acceptable and unacceptable questions

	Yes	No
1. May you ask: 'What is your mother tongue?'		
2. May you ask: 'What do you do in your spare time?'		
3. May you ask: 'Will you need to take special religious holidays?'		
4. May you reject an Asian candidate because you gathered evidence during the interview that he or she had bad personal hygiene?		
5. May you ask a female candidate whether her husband's job is in the near future likely to require him to relocate to another city?		
6. May you ask: 'How does your partner feel about the fact that this job will require you to travel abroad for potentially 50 per cent of the time?'		
7. Can you reject someone who is much older than the other employees who are currently doing the job in your organisation?		
8. May you ask: 'Have you ever been arrested?'		
9. Can you reject an ethnic minority candidate because he or she had poor spoken English skills?		
10. May you ask: 'What are the career aspirations of your partner?'		
11. May you ask a disabled candidate: 'Given your disability, how much time will you need off work?'		
12. May you reject a candidate who is much younger than you were expecting to hire for being 'emotionally immature'?		
13. May you ask: 'Please tell me about the organisations, clubs and societies that you belong to'?		

	Yes	No
14. May you ask: 'What sort of childcare provision do you have if we were to ask you to work late at short notice?'		
15. May you ask a candidate: 'Where does your family come from?'		

Let's take each of those questions in turn and see how you did. Now, remember not to shoot the messenger. I did not write the rules on what you should and should not ask. I am only reporting on what governments around the world have decided with regard to employment law:

1. No, you may not ask 'What is your mother tongue?' because it is not a job-related question. If, for example, you need someone who speaks fluent French, you could ask: 'What level of French do you possess?' or 'Are you able to speak in perfect colloquial French?' You could even test their French by asking them to answer questions in French or to complete some spoken or written test in French. But whether someone is French by birth or actually British or German or Chinese is irrelevant. The only question for job purposes that is relevant is their level of French.
2. No, you may not ask 'What do you do in your spare time?' Neither should you ask 'What are your hobbies?' as that could land you in hot water too. Again, these are not job-related questions. Employment law says that you should only ask questions that are related to a candidate's ability to do the job. Whether you personally find them an interesting person or not is not job-related. So whether candidates spend all of their time playing computer games or competitive team sports is not relevant to the job. A more effective and therefore permissible question would be 'What hobbies or interests do you have that might help you perform in this role?' However, an even better solution would be to ask only competency-based questions.

For example, if you wanted to find out if someone is a good team player, rather than asking whether they engage in solitary versus team-oriented hobbies, you should ask a question that directly relates to teamwork, such as 'Tell me about a time when you made a significant contribution to a team' or 'Talk me through a situation in which you...'

3. No, you may not ask 'Will you need to take special religious holidays?', as this question clearly asks whether a candidate has certain religious beliefs. You must assume that if certain candidates wish to apply for certain days of the year as holiday, they will do so as any employee might.
4. Yes, you can reject an Asian candidate for poor personal hygiene *so long as good personal hygiene is a requirement of the job* (eg the role is customer facing and the candidate has very strong body odour). This is a bit of a trick question as you can reject *any* candidate for bad personal hygiene irrespective of their ethnicity. However, remember that this must be a job-related requirement.
5. No, you should not ask a female candidate whether her husband's job is likely to require him to relocate. The reason this is a discriminatory question is because interviewers would rarely (if ever) ask the same question of a male candidate. By asking the question, you are making the assumption that the husband's job is more important than the wife's. Your interview questions can only focus on a candidate's competence and ability to do the job. You must not ask questions about candidates' personal lives.
6. Again, you should not ask this question because it probes into a candidate's personal life outside work. From a legal point of view, you must only test candidates' ability to do the job and allow them to make the decision as to whether they should take the job.
7. No, you may not reject candidates who are much older than the norm for a particular role. Age discrimination laws now state that interviewers should consider candidates of all ages for all jobs. So it is now illegal to state preferred age ranges or to reject people for being either too old or too young.

8. No, you may not ask about whether someone has been arrested. It is permissible to ask 'Have you been convicted of any crimes?' but not to ask about arrests. For example, people are occasionally arrested by the police but never charged because the police got it wrong. So you must not discriminate against people for merely having been arrested.
9. Yes, you can reject an ethnic minority candidate for poor spoken English skills. Again (as with question 4), this is a trick question. You can reject *any* candidate for having poor spoken English if having good spoken English is a requirement of the job.
10. No, you may not ask this question, as it is not directly relevant to the candidate's ability to do the job.
11. No, you may not ask a disabled candidate whether they might need time off work. It is unacceptable to ask *any* question that requires any candidate to talk about handicaps or health conditions that do not relate to the ability to do the job.
12. Yes, you may reject a candidate who is much younger than you were expecting to hire for being 'emotionally immature'. But then you could reject a 40- or 50-year-old candidate for being 'emotionally immature' so long as 'emotional maturity' is a requirement of the job. So long as you are rejecting a candidate for their level of skill rather than their absolute age, you are on safe ground.
13. No, you should not ask about the organisations, clubs and societies that a candidate belongs to. A candidate might reveal that he or she is a member of a union or a lesbian community group or a club for single fathers. This is not an acceptable question even if you wanted to test a candidate's networking skills. If you want to ask about networking skills, ask questions such as 'Give me an example of how you have used your personal network to benefit your employer's organisation' or 'Tell me about a time when you used your external network of contacts to gain a competitive advantage at work.'

14. No, you may not ask about childcare provision and a candidate's ability to work late. From a legal perspective, you must trust that the candidate understands the requirements of the job and will sort out childcare as appropriate. Your task during an interview can only be to find the most skilled person for the job.
15. No, you may not ask about a candidate's parents or ancestry because they are not related to the job.

The laws governing the interview process and what is legal or illegal are complex and could fill a book by themselves. However, the point is that you should focus only on questions that are directly relevant to the vacancy you are trying to fill. Asking questions that are only tangentially linked to the job could leave you open to discrimination lawsuits.

Acceptable and unacceptable questions

Table 4.2 outlines questions that are acceptable and unacceptable with regard to different areas of a candidate's life.

It may appear to list many questions that you cannot ask. However, you do not need to memorise them. There are two tips that will help you to avoid asking questions that may be discriminatory and therefore illegal:

1. Only ever ask questions that are directly related to a candidate's ability to perform the job.
2. Create an interview plan and work out the questions you wish to ask before the actual interview. You are far less likely to ask a discriminatory question by mistake if you plan your interview questions than if you simply turn up to interview a candidate without having thought through what you wish to ask.

Table 4.2 Acceptable and unacceptable questions

Topic	Unacceptable	Acceptable
General	What is your maiden name? What social or political organisations do you belong to?	What is your full name? Tell me how you have networked for the benefit of your organisation
Family and relations	Are you living with anyone? Do you live by yourself? What is your marital status? What is the name of your partner? What does your partner think of your work? Are you married, divorced, separated, living with someone, or single? Do you intend to get married soon? How many people live in your household? What does your father/mother do? How many siblings do you have?	What are the names of your relatives already employed by this company?
Pregnancy and children	Do you have children? Do you plan on having any more children? What are your long-term plans for family? What do you use for birth control? What are the names of your children? How old are your children? What childcare arrangements do you have in place?	Do you foresee any long-term absences in the future? Can you work overtime when needed? Can you work weekends? Can you do shift work? Is there any reason you could not start work at 7.00 am on certain days of the week?

	Who takes care of your children when you're at work? Who could take care of your children if they fell ill suddenly?	
Ethnicity, race, and nationality	What is your mother tongue? Where were you born? What country are you from? Where are your parents from? Would working with people of another race be a problem? What language is spoken in your home?	Do you have the necessary permits to work in this country? What languages do you speak, read, or write fluently?*
Age	How old are you? When were you born? How many years has it been since you left school/ university? How old are your children? Would you have difficulty working for a boss who is younger than you?	Are you at least 18 years of age?
Religion	Do you believe in God? What religious holidays do you observe? What do you do on Sundays? What is your religious affirmation? What groups are you a member of outside of work?	This job requires you to work on occasional weekends – will that be a problem for you?
Sexual orientation	What is your sexual orientation? What social organisations do you belong to? Are you straight? Are you gay?	None

Health and disability	What health problems do you have? How much do you weigh? Do you have any disabilities? Do you have any handicaps? What is the prognosis on your handicap? Have you ever been denied health insurance? When was the last time you saw a doctor?	Are you capable of performing the essenial responsibilities of the job? What special accommodations would you need to perform the job you have applied for?

*However, you may only ask this question if language skills are *directly* related to the job.

Stress and 'killer' questions

Some interviewers like to put candidates under pressure either by behaving negatively towards candidates (eg staring at them, talking over them, or demeaning their responses) or by asking aggressive questions such as the following:

- 'With your lack of relevant experience, why on earth do you think we should give you this job?'
- 'How would you respond if I said you're the worst candidate I've seen so far?'
- 'Are you good under pressure? What do you get if you multiply 37 by 11?'
- 'Our work requires a lot of quick thinking. See this pen I'm holding? Give me five reasons I might need a new one.'

These interviewers believe that treating candidates in such a way can help them to test candidates' reactions to stress. Unfortunately, such behaviour is disrespectful and you may find that the best candidates – the ones you most want to recruit – may simply decide that they would rather not work for your organisation. Neither do such questions test candidates' ability to react under proper, on-the-job pressure. You are unlikely to be looking for someone with the specific skills of being able to multiply numbers in their head without a calculator or persuade you to get a new pen.

If you are looking to test a candidate's ability to perform under pressure, rephrase your questions by asking for examples of stressful situations they have been in. Consider, for example:

- 'Please talk me through an occasion in which you had to prioritise your work when working under pressure.'
- 'Tell me about a time when you dealt with a stressful situation.'
- 'Tell me about the rudest colleague or customer you've had to deal with in the last year.'

Pop psychology questions

Interviewers sometimes try to delve into the psyches of candidates by asking apparently deep or philosophical questions such as:

- 'What do you do when you feel lonely?'
- 'If you were a cartoon character, who would you be and why?'
- 'What's your favourite time of year and why?'
- 'If you could throw a dinner party for six people from any time in history, who would you invite and why would you invite them?'

Interviewers often adopt pop psychology questions that they have heard other interviewers ask and occasionally even questions that they themselves were asked in previous job interviews.

Trust me (I'm a chartered psychologist) when I say that such questions have little or no value. Candidates tend to try to second-guess what you want to hear as opposed to telling you what they really think. In any case, what you believe to be the 'right' or 'wrong' answer may not be what a reputable psychologist or even another interviewer within your own organisation may deem 'right' or 'wrong'.

Hypothetical questions

Hypothetical questions are open questions that ask candidates to consider hypothetical scenarios or situations. Examples include:

- 'How do you think you would feel if you failed to meet your sales targets for the year?'
- 'How would you cope if two customers asked to meet you on the same day and at the same time?'
- 'How would you go about organising a complex project?'

Many hypothetical questions are of little use because they are too transparent – candidates can often second-guess what the right answer should be. Most candidates try to tell you what they *think* you would want them to do or feel in that situation rather than tell you what they would actually do or feel.

So, in answer to the first example question, you might expect most candidates to respond that they would feel awful about missing their targets and would therefore work harder to achieve them. Most candidates would respond to the second question by saying that they'd try to negotiate with both customers to reschedule the meeting. And in answer to the third question, candidates might explain how they would put together a project plan, consult relevant people, establish realistic deadlines for different parts of the project, and so on. But in selecting someone for a job, wouldn't you rather hire someone who can talk about how they *had* tackled complex projects in the past rather than someone who had never organised a project and could talk only about how they would *in theory* do it?

Remember that what candidates *say* they would do could be

completely different from what they would *actually* do. As such, rather than asking hypothetical questions about what they might do, the better approach would be to ask for actual examples that allow you to see how they really behaved. So, the above three questions would therefore become:

- 'Tell me about the last time you missed or failed to achieve a target.'
- 'Talk me through a situation in which you had to deal with two competing demands.'
- 'Talk us through how you went about organising a particularly complex project.'

Leading questions

Be careful not to ask questions that suggest to the candidate what the right answer should be. Such questions are pointless, as almost all candidates will simply tell you what they think you want to hear. Consider these examples of leading questions:

- 'Time management is very important in this job. Are you good at managing your time?'
- 'Do you mind doing overtime?'
- 'Do you think it's important to work together as a team to achieve results?'

A far better approach to ask about the skills of time management, demonstrating dedication to the job, and teamwork would be to rephrase those questions. Consider instead the following questions that ask about previous situations in which the candidate had to demonstrate those skills:

- 'Give me an example of an occasion when you had to manage your time.'
- 'When was the last time you had to work late or do overtime? Tell me about it.'

- 'Talk me through a time when you had to work closely in a team in order to achieve a result.'

Multiple questions

A multiple question is a string of questions that bombards candidates with too much information for them to take in at once. Consider the following examples:

- 'Tell me about a time you exceeded your line manager's expectations. Then explain when this happened, how it came about, what his or her expectations were, how you responded, and what you learnt from the situation.'
- 'Why did you choose the degree subject and university that you chose? How do you feel it has prepared you for the real world of work? What do you still feel you need to learn? And what are your intentions with regard to doing further courses of study in the future?'

As you can see, such questions may confuse a candidate. It would be far better to break each of these multiple questions down into individual interview funnels. So ask the first question, listen to the response, then ask the next question, and so on. By asking only one question at a time, you can ensure that a candidate will not get confused by the question, forget some part of it, or try to get away with answering only the easiest part of it.

Self-assessment questions

Self-assessment questions ask candidates to assess themselves. Examples include:

- 'What are your strengths?'
- 'What are your weaknesses?'

- ‘On a scale of one to ten, how good are you at coping in a crisis?’
- ‘How good are your people skills?’
- ‘Describe your character.’

These questions have little value because candidates will simply give you an answer that tries to sell their skills. All you are testing is their way with words rather than understanding their actual strengths or weaknesses, how good they are at coping in a crisis, the extent of their people skills, and so on.

In particular, when asking questions about a candidate’s weaknesses, all you are testing is whether they have memorised what they believe to be a good model answer. They may reply that they are ‘perfectionists’ or ‘don’t suffer fools gladly’. But these are just responses learnt by rote rather than replies that touch on their real weaknesses.

What often happens is that it is the most deluded candidates who give the most flowery and overly positive assessments of themselves. If you know the competencies that you are looking for, the better approach is to ask for examples of situations in which candidates demonstrated those competencies rather than asking candidates to evaluate themselves.

General questions

Competency-based interviewing is designed to probe specific incidents that have already happened. Be careful to ensure that your questions are therefore always phrased in the past tense.

Be watchful not to ask questions that ask for a candidate to talk about how they *generally* deal with different situations, such as:

- ‘How do you deal with difficult customers?’
- ‘What’s your approach to making tough decisions?’
- ‘How do you go about changing someone’s mind?’

In order to test a candidate's past behaviour, those three questions should therefore be rephrased as follows:

- 'Tell me about a time when you dealt with a difficult customer.'
- 'Talk me through an occasion when you had to make a tough decision.'
- 'Tell me about a particular time when you changed someone's mind.'

Overly broad questions

There are some very broad questions that might be useful in the first few minutes of the interview for encouraging candidates to talk about themselves, such as:

- 'Tell me about yourself.'
- 'What are you most proud of?'
- 'What regrets do you have?'

Avoid asking questions that are too broad in their scope as they rarely provide useful evidence against which you can judge candidates. For example, in answer to the first question, I have had candidates respond by talking about where they were born, raised, went to school, got a first job, and so on. In answer to the second question, I have had candidates tell me about personal achievements such as bringing up a family, stopping smoking, losing weight, and so on. In terms of regrets, candidates have talked about topics including divorces, losing touch with family members, and so on. None of those answers are technically wrong given the broad nature of the questions. But it would be a better use of your time to ask more specific questions that relate directly to the job such as:

- 'Tell me about your current job' (and only use this question to provide context before moving on to more specific competency-based questions).

- 'What project are you most proud of from the last year?' (and then lead into asking when it happened, what the candidate did, and so on – to test a competency).
- 'Tell me about a mistake you made at work and how you dealt with it' (which would provide you with evidence about how candidates deal with mistakes – if that were an important competency for the vacancy you are trying to fill).

Questions about fit

Most organisations have their own distinctive culture, so it is unsurprising that managers often want to hire candidates who 'fit' into their culture. When managers talk about 'fit', they often refer to qualities such as teamwork, taking the initiative, attitudes to risk, the need for reward, and so on. Typical questions that try to measure fit may go as follows:

- 'How do you operate as a team player?'
- 'Do you prefer to communicate by e-mail, memo, telephone or in person?'
- 'What do you do when things are slow at work?'
- 'What kind of team would you like to work for?'
- 'Do you prefer working alone or with others?'
- 'How do you like to be rewarded for a good job?'

However, these questions are rarely the best ways to gauge whether candidates are likely to fit into your culture. Candidates will of course try to tell you what they think the right answer is – you have no way of assessing whether candidates actually believe what they are telling you or whether they are simply second-guessing what they think you want to hear.

A far better alternative is to ask for examples of situations in which candidates have behaved in the ways you would like them to behave. For example, if your organisation stresses initiative and autonomy over teamwork, ask a question such as: 'Tell me about a time when you demonstrated autonomy and worked independently of other people in your team.' On the other hand, if your organisation is very team oriented, then ask: 'Give me an example of a situation in which you achieved a goal as an integral part of a team.'

Consider as another example candidates' attitudes to reward. Rather than asking how candidates like to be rewarded for their work, ask a question in the past tense such as: 'Tell me about a time when you felt rewarded in your work.' By turning questions about fit into questions phrased in the past tense that ask about behaviour, you can more accurately gauge whether candidates have in the past demonstrated the behaviours that would allow them to fit into your team.

5

Honing your listening skills

Body language and voice

How you behave and your tone of voice can have a large impact on your ability to draw information effectively from a candidate. If you come across as distant and aloof, you could reduce the amount of information that candidates are willing to share with you. Taken to its extreme, even otherwise strong candidates could decide not to elaborate on their experience because they have decided that they don't like you and don't want to work for your organisation.

I've already mentioned (see Chapter 3) that the best way to find the most suitable candidate for the job is by putting all candidates at ease to ensure that you can get them to talk openly about their experience. Good interviewers encourage candidates to talk and demonstrate that they are paying attention by using a technique called 'active listening'. Consider these tips to ensure that you put your candidates at ease:

- Make eye contact with candidates whenever possible. In order to convey interest and sincerity, aim to maintain eye contact in bursts of between 5 and 10 seconds before looking away each time. Less than 5 seconds communicates either lack of interest or nervousness; significantly more than 10 seconds could be misread as staring. Do by all means look down at your pre-prepared interview plan to remind yourself of questions you need to ask. Do also look at your notepad when you are writing notes on what candidates are saying. But otherwise try to glance up from your notes to look candidates in the eyes as much as possible.

- Nod your head occasionally to encourage the candidate to continue speaking.
- Use words, phrases and sounds such as 'yes', 'that makes sense', 'uh-huh', 'go on', or whatever you feel is appropriate to show that you are paying attention.
- Mirror a candidate's facial expressions as appropriate. For example, if a candidate tells you about an exciting time that he or she experienced, it may be appropriate to smile. If a candidate tells you about an unpleasant work situation or difficult personal circumstances, you may decide to be somewhat less upbeat to show that you empathise with how he or she felt.
- Sit upright or lean towards the candidate when he or she is speaking. Slouching or leaning back could be seen as signs of indifference.

At the same time, be careful to avoid negative body language such as:

- looking repeatedly at your watch or out of a window (which could be interpreted as boredom);
- fidgeting with your hands;
- frowning;
- pointing your finger at the candidate (which could be perceived as unnecessarily aggressive);
- creating barriers such as by crossing your arms or sitting behind a large desk.

Interjecting

Remember that the main purpose of the interview is to gather evidence as to the extent that different candidates meet the requirements of the job. If candidates go off track and begin to give you examples or opinions that do not allow you to judge their suitability for the role (eg not talking specifically about their actions and/or giving too much background or other less relevant information), it is your job to stop them politely and steer them back on course.

As the interviewer, you must feel confident enough to speak up if you feel that a candidate is going off track. It helps if you warn candidates in your introduction at the start of the interview that you may interrupt occasionally (see Chapter 7 and also the worked example in Chapter 3). Once you have given them prior notice that you may interject, it allows you to steer them back onto relevant topics by using phrases such as:

- 'Thank you for that. Can I ask...?'
- 'Can I stop you there? I did mention that I would interrupt and that's all I need on that topic. Can we move on to...?'
- 'Apologies but my original question was...'
- 'Can I stop you for a moment and ask...?'
- 'Sorry to interrupt, but can I ask...?'
- 'I think I understand enough of the background, could you take me through the actions you took to deal with it, please?'

To make it easier to stop candidates while they are speaking, use your body language to signal that you want to interject. For example, if you are taking notes, try putting down your pen and raising your hand to show that you want to speak.

If you find that you repeatedly have to interject for the same reason, you may wish to give some form of feedback to the candidate to guide him or her as to what you are looking for. Depending on what the candidate is doing wrong, consider using phrases such as:

- 'I understand that you want to give me a lot of the background, but can I assure you that I need only a small amount of context? Could I ask you to focus on *your* particular contribution, please?'
- 'Can I stop you for a second and remind you that I'm most interested in specific examples rather than talking in general terms about how you handle such situations? Take a few seconds if you need to come up with just one specific example, please.'
- 'It would help me if you begin each example with just a little bit more background first so that I can understand why you chose to deal with each situation in the way you did.'

Learning to interject is one of the biggest challenges facing interviewers. Most interviewers feel reluctant to interrupt – certainly most books on listening skills advise you to avoid interrupting people as they are speaking. However, remember that this is an interview in which you are trying to collect evidence about the candidate's behaviour within a limited time.

Remember, never be worried about interrupting a candidate when you need to. Having the confidence to stop and redirect a candidate who is not giving you useful evidence is the sign of a *good* interviewer. But do bear in mind that interrupting is not about cutting rudely into what candidates are saying; simply stop candidates and redirect them by asking whatever question you need to ask. And do it with an appropriately gentle tone of voice and with a smile – explaining what you want from candidates does not have to be at all impolite or abrasive.

Taking notes

I've mentioned several times already that an interview is about collecting evidence as to the extent to which each candidate is a good fit for the job. And in order to capture that evidence, I would strongly advise you to take written notes. Do not rely on your memory. No matter how good you think your memory is, I can guarantee you that the details of what each candidate said will blur with the passing of even just a few hours.

At the same time, writing notes shows to candidates very visibly that you are paying attention to what they are saying; taking notes helps candidates to feel that what they are saying is important and has value.

The best option is to have a separate note taker – someone who can simply write down what the candidate is saying. This leaves you, the interviewer, free to focus on building a rapport and thinking about your next question. However, this is obviously more resource-intensive and few organisations have the luxury of dedicated note takers.

Whether it falls to you or some other person to take notes, you should warn candidates beforehand that you will be taking notes to help you remember exactly what is discussed during the interview. If nothing else, announcing your intentions is simply polite (see also Chapter 7).

Recording the interview (either sound or sound and vision) is an alternative. However, it can be quite off-putting to candidates, and interviewers then have to spend even more time listening to or watching what was recorded in order to evaluate the evidence. As such, recording interviews is rarely used in practice.

Verbatim comments

When writing interview notes, avoid evaluating or interpreting what is being said. Try to take notes that represent what was actually said – as close as possible to a verbatim transcript of what the candidate is saying. For example, if a candidate says 'I rang the client and promised her that I'd deliver the package myself if it didn't turn up in the next 24 hours', then write that down (or as much of it as you can) rather than writing down 'spoke to client and made her happy'. The detail may be important at a later date and unless you try to capture the detail during the interview, it will get blurred in your memory with the passing of time.

Of course, avoid taking notes that are so comprehensive that you have to stop continually and at length throughout the interview, breaking eye contact and destroying any rapport. However, if there is something of particular interest that you want to capture, do not be afraid occasionally to leave a brief pause after the candidate has answered one question before you ask the next one.

Avoid writing down only what you think is important at the time. It can be difficult to know what is important until after the interview is over. You could find that something apparently trivial that you decided not to write down at the time could later become important when the candidate gives you further information. As a rule, write it down first; evaluate it later.

Notes as a legal document

Be aware that your handwritten notes become a legal document. Organisations are expected to keep all handwritten notes for at least several years in case of legal challenges over hiring decisions. So writing any inappropriate comments about a candidate such as 'stupid' or 'unattractive' could have legal consequences. Even writing a comment such as 'the American candidate' or 'blonde lady' with the honest intention of helping you to remember who the candidate was could be interpreted in a court of law as evidence of discrimination.

6

Preparing to interview

Recruiting possible candidates

The terms 'recruitment' and 'selection' are often used together. However, when defined properly, they actually have slightly different meanings. Recruitment is the process of attracting a large pool of candidates and making them sufficiently interested to put themselves forward for consideration for the job. Selection is the process of sorting through the interested candidates and identifying the right ones to hire for the job. As such, organisations must first recruit candidates before they can select from them.

Attracting the right candidates

Most organisations recruit candidates by using some combination of:

- advertising their vacancies in the national and/or local press or through professional and trade publications;
- advertising their vacancies online via specialist job sites as well as their own corporate website;
- attending exhibitions and career conventions;

- employing the services of recruitment agencies and executive search firms (often known as 'headhunters');
- relying on word-of-mouth referrals via employees or contacts and acquaintances outside of the organisation;
- advertising opportunities internally to existing employees across the organisation as well as externally.

The purpose of recruitment is not just to attract *any* candidates – it is to recruit the *right* candidates (and hopefully put off the wrong sort of candidates). For example, organisations with a high public profile often find that they are inundated with applications from all sorts of candidates – many of whom do not have the right skills, experience or motivation. Similarly, some jobs in seemingly exciting sectors such as advertising, fashion, media and entertainment also receive many applications simply because candidates believe that the jobs are highly desirable – many of the candidates again lack the right experience, skills, motivation or proper understanding of the nature of the work to make good employees.

Compare the phrasing of the two advertisements for the same job as a junior researcher within a television production company (Table 6.1). The positive job advertisement makes the job sound incredibly enticing; the organisation is likely to be bombarded with applications from all sorts of candidates – some of whom may be far less suitable than others. The more realistic job advertisement points out some of the skills that are required as well as some of the downsides. It is unlikely that candidates who hate spending time on the telephone or who wish only to work predictable hours would apply for the job on the basis of the realistic job advertisement.

Having too many unsuitable candidates apply for the job may mean that more time and resources have to be devoted to sifting CVs and covering letters or application forms. As such, it is important to present an accurate picture of the job and the organisation (sometimes called a 'realistic job preview') – by highlighting the genuinely good aspects of working for the organisation, but at the same time also pointing out some of the realistic downsides of the job as well. To help candidates

Table 6.1 Comparison of an overly positive and a more realistic job advertisement

Positive	Realistic
An exciting opportunity for a dynamic graduate to join a TV production company as a junior researcher. You will be working as part of a fun team to put together programming for broadcast on the major television channels. As well as occasionally meeting and working alongside TV presenters and celebrities, you will find yourself being thrown into all sorts of thrilling situations. The junior researcher role is the first step on the career ladder that could lead you to running your own television production company! Call 060 8901 7456 for an application form.	An oppportunity for a graduate to join a TV production company as a junior researcher. Key requirements include: ■ Experience of using the telephone for work and/or research purposes. ■ Ability to research quickly and effectively using the internet. ■ Strong oral and written presentation skills, with the ability to present ideas and data to colleagues. ■ Willingness to work unpredictable hours and occasional weekends as necessary. Call 060 8901 7456 for an application form.

understand the true nature of the job, many organisations either advertise using a shortened version of the person specification or even provide all of the person specification (perhaps online or by offering to send it out to interested parties).

Methods of application

Once potential candidates have been alerted to vacancies within the organisation, they are typically asked to apply by submitting either a curriculum vitae (CV) and a covering letter, or an application form created by the organisation.

The main difference between a CV and an application form is in the party that has control over what information is presented. In a CV, the candidate decides what to reveal (and what to avoid sharing); in an application form, the organisation asks candidates what the organisation wants to know. An application form may take you more time to design than simply asking for a CV and covering letter, but it will ensure you find out exactly what you need to know.

Whichever application method your organisation decides to use, you can check candidates' backgrounds and immediately reject candidates who do not possess the qualifications or experience that you need. You can then decide on the candidates you want to invite to interview.

Preparing a shortlist

Aim to create a shortlist of between three and eight candidates per vacancy to bring to interview. Having a shortlist of fewer than three candidates may restrict your chances of finding a candidate who is good enough for the job; having a shortlist of significantly greater than eight candidates is likely to put a strain on the interviewers' and organisation's time.

Designing the interview process

Before you bring candidates in for interview, you first need to decide what the interview process will consist of. You will need to decide on answers to the following five questions:

- How many rounds or stages of interview should there be? Consider whether you will invite candidates to come to your organisation on only one day or on more than one day. Each separate day is considered one round.
- How many interviews should there be in each round? Think about whether you need only one interview per round or perhaps several interviews per round.

- Who should interview the candidates? How many managers and/or supervisors are trained in interviewing and need to meet the candidates?
- How many interviewers should attend each interview? For example, if you have quite a few rounds of interviews, it may be appropriate to have one-to-one interviews. If you have fewer rounds but still need to have many managers meet each candidate, you may want a panel interview at some stage.
- How long should each interview be? Consider the trade-off between how much information you need to collect versus how much time you want to spend interviewing.

The answers to these questions are likely to depend on the seniority and/or importance of the role. For example, if you were looking to hire a new junior administrator to join the team, you might be able to get away with only one interview by the person who will become the successful candidate's direct supervisor. On the other hand, if you were hiring a senior manager, you might wish to have several rounds of one-to-one interviews as well as a panel interview consisting of a handful of people who have a stake in the appointment.

Consider also the following factors in deciding what your interview process should look like:

- the number of vacancies there are to fill;
- the number of applications you are likely to receive – will it be only a handful or in the hundreds (or even thousands)?
- the resources (eg number of interviewers as well as number of interview rooms) you have available to you;
- the date by which you need to have appointed someone to the role (and therefore the amount of time you have to complete the overall interview process).

Figure 6.1 presents the selection process for a large national organisation aiming to hire four new graduate trainees from several hundred applications. Figure 6.2 presents a very simple process for a local organisation hiring a new personal assistant

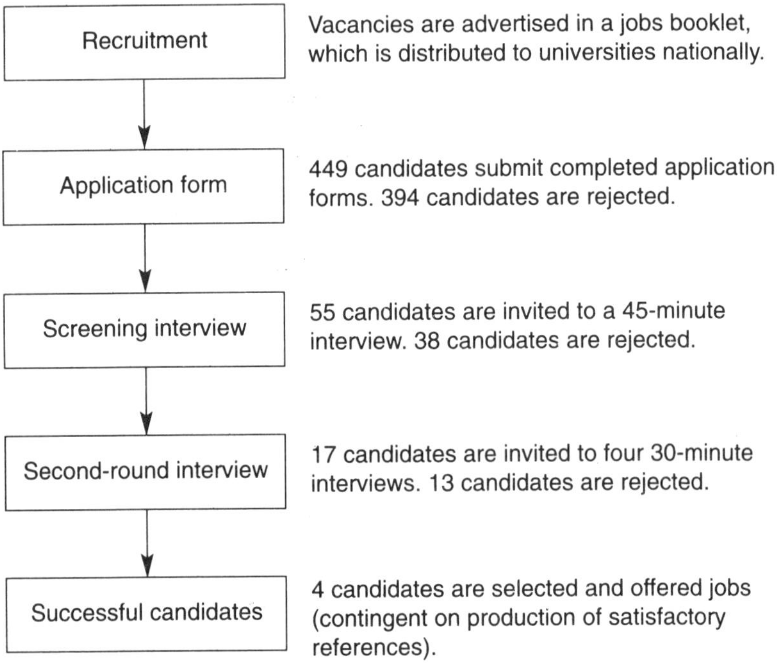

Figure 6.1 Example of a selection process aiming to hire four graduate trainees.

from only several dozen applications. Figure 6.3 presents the process for hiring one senior director. As you can see from these examples, there can be many variations on the number of rounds of interviewing, number of interviews per round, the length of each interview, and so on.

It is difficult to apply firm rules in deciding what an interview process should look like. However, consider the following rules of thumb:

- **Allow *at least* 10 minutes (and usually closer to 15 minutes) to investigate each competency.** If you want to probe six competencies, you would either need at least one 60-minute interview (although preferably a 90-minute

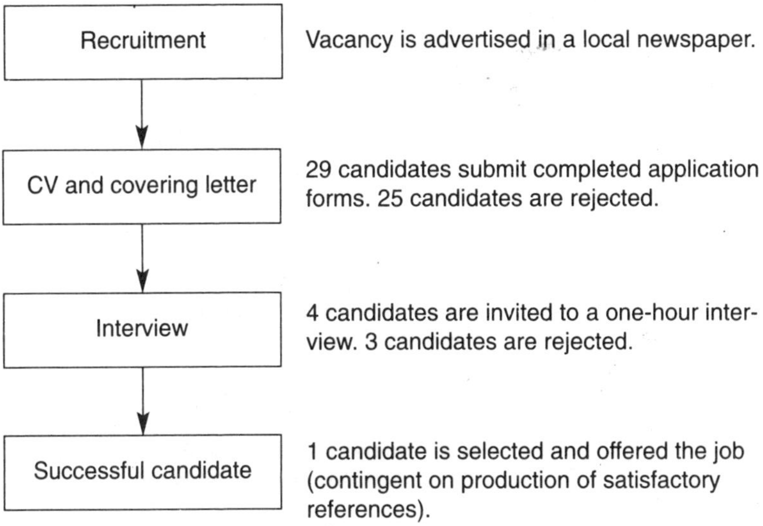

Figure 6.2 Example of a selection process aiming to hire a personal assistant.

interview) or perhaps two half-hour interviews run by different interviewers.

- **Aim to reduce the total pool of candidates after each round of interviewing.** Aim to invite back somewhere in the region of between 1 in 3 and 1 in 5 candidates for each successive round. For example, say your interview process consists of two rounds. If you had a dozen candidates to begin with, you should aim to invite back only around 3, 4 (or at most 5) candidates to the second and final round of interviewing.
- **Ask different questions during each interview.** There is little point in taking candidates through the same questions. As such, think about different questions you can use to probe further candidates' strengths and shortcomings. Even if you are probing the same competencies in different interviews, think of different questions to ask each time.

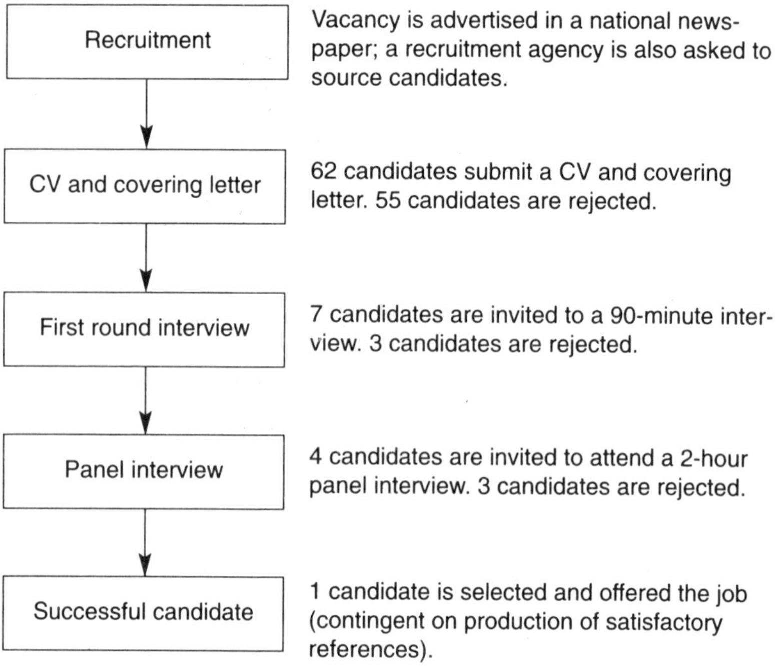

Figure 6.3 Example of a selection process aiming to hire one IT director.

- **Keep early rounds of interviews briefer.** Say you are meeting university undergraduates on campus in order to decide which ones to invite back to your offices for a lengthier interview. Each first-round interview might reasonably consist of only half an hour to check that candidates have basic social skills and at least some understanding about your graduate programme; later rounds might last longer and be more in-depth.
- **Have as few rounds as possible.** If you need to have more than one interview, the best way to structure an interview day is to have a number of back-to-back interviews. In this way, candidates who are currently holding jobs can minimise the amount of time they take away from their jobs.

Inviting candidates to interview

Once you have decided on the candidates to put on your shortlist and the shape of your overall interview process, you can begin to invite candidates to interview. Bear in mind that candidates may have other diary commitments so try to give candidates at least several weeks' notice. Many organisations first telephone candidates to arrange a mutually agreeable time and date for the interview and then follow up with a letter to confirm details such as:

- time and date of interview;
- length of interview;
- location of interview;
- details of any documents or samples candidates may need to bring along, such as:
  - qualification certificates;
  - proof of residence or eligibility to work;
  - examples of work such as a portfolio of artwork, photographs or other materials if they are directly relevant to the job (eg as an artist, photographer and so on);
  - driving licence (for jobs that require driving);
- name(s) of interviewer(s).

Interviewing with colleagues

Having one or more colleagues join you during interviews can help you to interview more effectively:

- Other interviewers can listen, observe, and take notes while you are asking questions (and vice versa).
- Different interviewers tend to remember different parts of the interview, so your combined recollection afterwards will be more complete.
- The presence of other interviewers can protect you from claims of unfair discrimination.

It is an especially good idea to have colleagues interview alongside each other when there are novice interviewers who may need some support from more experienced interviewers. However, having multiple interviewers present of course means that the process becomes much more resource intensive.

Ground rules

If you intend to interview with one or more colleagues, you should get together beforehand to discuss ground rules for how to handle the interview, otherwise you could end up speaking over each other or even forgetting to cover certain topics. Consider:

- Which interviewer will speak first in introducing the interview?
- Who is going to take notes? Will one interviewer write notes while the other is speaking? Or will each interviewer take their own notes?
- Which topics or areas will each interviewer cover? And in what order will the interviewers cover those areas? For example, will one interviewer ask questions for the first half of the interview or will each interviewer take it in turn to ask a question?
- Who will close the interview?

There is no single best way to handle an interview with multiple interviewers. Decide on the approach that will work best for the interviewers. However, avoid playing 'good cop, bad cop' in which one interviewer is friendly and another is hostile – such an approach not only fails to gather more useful information but also comes across as unprofessional.

Panel interviews

A panel interview (also sometimes called a board interview) can be useful if multiple decision-makers within the organisation need to be involved in selecting the right candidate for a (usually more senior) job. A typical panel might consist of the immediate supervisor, a representative from human resources, and perhaps representatives from other departments that would be impacted by the new hire.

When interviewing as a panel, be aware that panel interviews tend to be quite formal and can be quite intimidating to candidates. In fact, the more people there are on the panel, the more difficult it can be to put candidates at ease and encourage them to talk freely. As such, ensure that all of the people who attend a panel *need* (as opposed to want) to be there.

Scheduling

If you are seeing multiple candidates on the same day, be careful not to book too many interviews in at once. Make sure you leave adequate time between interviews to:

- write up notes on the last candidate;
- familiarise yourself with the next candidate;
- take a comfort break.

If you have not done much interviewing before, also be aware that many interviewers try to pack too many questions into an interview and end up overrunning. As a rule of thumb, aim to leave at least 15 minutes between interviews – even better if you can leave half an hour between them.

Think also about the needs of your candidates. If candidates are being asked to attend multiple interviews over the course of the day, you may need to provide them with lunch and/or time for comfort breaks too. If your candidates are very senior (and therefore may know each other from having worked in the same industry for any length of time), bear in mind that it may also be inappropriate for them to bump into each other, so think of ways to keep them separated.

Setting up the room

Spending a few minutes setting up the interview room not only helps you to interview more effectively, but also helps to convey a professional demeanour to candidates.

Here are some tips on setting up the interview environment appropriately:

- Ensure that the interview room is sufficiently quiet (eg well sound-proofed). Put a sign on the outside of the door that says 'Interview in progress – please do not disturb'.
- Tell your colleagues not to put telephone calls through to that room and/or put the telephone on Do Not Disturb mode if it has one.
- Be ready to offer candidates a drink as they are likely to be doing most of the talking during the interview and may get a dry throat. Think about who will get the drink for the candidate – will it be yourself or one of your colleagues?
- Find some way to keep track of the time so that you do not fall behind on your interview schedule. Ideally, mount a clock on the wall behind the candidate so you can look at the clock without the candidate noticing.
- Have to hand copies of the candidate's CV, covering letter and/or application form, plus your interview plan.
- Have a notepad and pen ready for taking notes.
- Have to hand copies of any organisational literature or brochures that you wish to give to candidates.

Seating

Try to avoid sitting behind your desk if you can. Having a desk between yourself and a candidate can make the situation feel slightly confrontational from the candidate's perspective. If you can, try to sit on adjacent sides of a desk to create a more informal, friendly atmosphere.

Think also about the distance that separates you. If you set up the room so that you are sitting too close to someone, they will perceive you to be invading their personal space. If you are seated too far apart, you may struggle to build much rapport with each other, which could cause the interview to feel stilted and uncomfortable.

Interviewing on the move

An interview is supposed to be a two-way process. While there is of course a large part of the interview that is about you as an interviewer deciding which candidate you want to hire, there is also an element of allowing candidates to decide whether they would want to work for your organisation.

The traditional interview (ie sitting in a room around a table) can be augmented – but not replaced – by taking candidates on a tour around the organisation and allowing candidates to meet people that they would potentially have to interact with. In this way, candidates gain a better appreciation of what it would be like to work in the organisation – meeting the people, seeing more of the organisation's premises and working conditions, and soaking up the atmosphere. At the same time, you as an interviewer can judge how the candidate comes across in meeting important stakeholders across your organisation.

However, bear in mind that a roving interview should only be used to *supplement* the structured interview rather than replace it. It's difficult to ask penetrating questions during an interview on the move. At the same time, you will be hard pressed to take sufficiently detailed notes while on the move to allow you to compare different candidates at a later date.

Telephone interviewing

Telephone interviews are being used more frequently by organisations that need to hire large volumes of candidates for fairly junior roles. However, telephone interviews are unpopular with both candidates and line managers. Candidates dislike the fact that they cannot put their case across in person; line managers dislike having to make judgements as to whom to hire without seeing candidates face-to-face.

You may wish to interview over the telephone if you are looking to hire a large number of fairly junior candidates and need to whittle down dozens or possibly hundreds of candidates into a more manageable number to invite to face-to-face interview. When using telephone interviews, consider the following points:

- Research shows that telephone interviews almost always result in lower ratings of candidates by interviewers. Therefore you should have a much lower than normal threshold or hurdle (see 'Setting a selection hurdle' in Chapter 11) to avoid eliminating genuinely good candidates.
- Telephone interviews should not be mixed with face-to-face interviews in the same round of the interview process. Given that telephone interviews usually result in lower ratings, it would be unfair to compare directly some candidates who were interviewed in person with others who were interviewed over the telephone.
- You should aim to be consistent in the questions that you ask in order to be fair to all candidates. A telephone interview should be no less structured than a face-to-face interview. Make sure you introduce the interview, ask competency-based questions, write down the evidence that you hear, and evaluate the evidence in the same way that you would for a face-to-face interview.

Interviewers are also increasingly interviewing candidates via videoconference and even webcam. Again, because it may be harder for candidates and interviewers to build a rapport with each other, bear in mind that it would be unfair to compare candidates who were interviewed face-to-face with candidates who were interviewed using technology.

The CV and covering letter

The candidate's CV and covering letter (and/or application form) have got the candidate to the point of being offered an interview. Perhaps you or one of your colleagues has decided that the candidate's skills and experiences match the requirements of the job – or at least they do on paper.

The beauty of competency-based interviewing is that you do not need a detailed knowledge of the candidate's CV. Rather than asking questions about specific periods of the candidate's career history (eg 'Tell me about a time you managed a budget when you worked for Perkins & Smith'), good competency-based questions should be much more open-ended (eg 'Tell me about a recent time you managed a budget').

As such, you do *not* need to memorise details about a candidate's CV. However, you may wish to study their CV to look out for issues such as:

- **Gaps in the CV**. If a candidate has been out of work for some time, you may wish to explore the reasons why. For example, did they voluntarily take time out to learn a craft or further their personal development? Were they simply unable to find work? Or are there any ongoing health issues that could prevent the candidate from fulfilling the requirements of the job for which you are interviewing them?
- **Changes of direction in the CV**. If, for example, the candidate has previously worked as a journalist and a sales representative, but is now applying to work for your organisation as a political researcher, you might well want to ask some questions about their motivation and career aspirations (see Chapter 10).
- **Any inconsistencies or possible exaggerations**. All candidates try to make their CV sound as good as possible – they want the job after all! So scan through the CV and look for potential inconsistencies and/or possible exaggerations. If you feel that anything does not ring true, think about what questions you could ask to confirm or disconfirm your suspicions.

7

Opening the interview

As a rule of thumb, aim to *spend around 70 to 80 per cent of your time during an interview asking competency-based questions* and investigating candidates' past behaviour. However, to begin with, you need to spend a few minutes putting candidates at ease and introducing yourself and the approach you will take during the rest of the interview.

Your frame of mind

It's human nature to form snap impressions – we all do it. But as an interviewer, you must be on your guard not to form judgements about candidates that may have little to do with their ability to do the job.

For example, one interviewer may dislike men who have long hair (or women with very short hair). Perhaps another interviewer has a more positive impression of graduates from certain universities (and a more negative impression of graduates from other universities). If we are not careful, we may ask tougher questions of candidates we have a negative bias against and easier questions of candidates we like. Irrespective of your first impressions, be careful to treat all candidates in a consistent and fair manner.

Putting candidates at ease

Research shows that the best way to find the most suitable candidate for the job is by putting all candidates at ease and allowing them to talk in a relaxed and comfortable way about their experiences and behaviour. How you do this is a matter for personal preference, but always begin an interview by at least greeting candidates warmly and introducing yourself.

Pronunciation of names

People hate to have their names mispronounced. Mispronouncing a name multiple times during an interview is almost sure to set a candidate on edge. If you are in any doubt as to the pronunciation of a candidate's first name – especially as the world becomes an increasingly multicultural place – make sure to ask at the very beginning of the interview.

Rapport, not hostility

There is a small minority of interviewers who deliberately try to put candidates under stress by asking questions in a hostile fashion in order to see how they might cope with stress on the job. However, research shows that a candidate who copes well with a stressful interview may not be very good at the job and vice versa. The best approach is always to put candidates at ease to ensure that you can get them to talk openly about their experience and the situations they have been in.

In order to strike up a rapport, it is worth spending a few minutes making small talk – either as you guide the candidate from reception to the interview room or in the interview room itself. Be warm and friendly and ask a few questions on neutral topics such as the candidate's journey, the weather, what they think of your office building, and so on.

Another technique for building rapport is by finding some common ground with which to break the ice. For example, you might spot something on a candidate's CV that allows you to make comment such as:

- 'I noticed you play the viola. I used to play the violin at school. Do you still play much?'
- 'I see you went to university in Bristol. I grew up there. How did you find your time at Bristol?'
- 'I saw from your CV that you like to read. Have you read anything recently that you'd recommend?'

You only need to use one or two such comments to get the candidate used to talking to you. Avoid making too many of these comments, otherwise the candidate could interpret it as the tone of the interview and see it as an opportunity to ramble at length on topics that are actually of no use to you.

Body language and tone of voice

I've already covered the use of body language during the interview. But think particularly about how you behave and your tone of voice in opening the interview. If you cannot help a candidate to relax quickly, you will not be able to gather evidence as effectively as possible.

Think about not only *what* you say, but also *how* you say it. Asking 'How was your journey?' in an aggressive tone with a scowl on your face and arms crossed tightly over your chest obviously conveys a very different impression than if you were to ask the same question while smiling warmly and adopting a light tone of voice.

Of course, you would never consciously leave a rude or indifferent impression on a candidate. But unless we make a conscious effort to think about our body language and tone of voice, we can all sometimes inadvertently stray into coming across inappropriately.

Handling lateness and other issues

You may sometimes come across candidates who arrive late and/or looking dishevelled. Of course this may have an impact on your assessment of candidates, but try to avoid letting it colour how you conduct the interview itself. Remember that the purpose of an interview is to *collect* evidence as to the candidate's suitability for a job – the time to evaluate the evidence and decide whether or not to hire a candidate comes after the interview has ended. Being late and/or scruffy is merely *one* piece of evidence. You should avoid making an issue of it and instead ask the questions that you had originally intended to ask in order to gather a full picture of the candidate's strengths and weaknesses.

If *you* arrive late, apologise only once. Avoid wasting more time by giving elaborate explanations and move straight into introducing the interview instead.

Introducing the interview

After no more than a few minutes of small talk, you should broach the subject of the interview. Your introduction should:

- introduce yourself and set the interview parameters (eg length of interview, number of interviewers);
- explain the interview approach (ie the style of a competency-based interview);
- check the candidate's understanding before you start.

Although you should by now have introduced yourself by name, you may wish to give the candidate a little bit more background on yourself and your role. If there are other interviewers who may be involved over the course of the day, you should mention this now as well. Finally, it is a matter of courtesy to mention the length of the interview and that you will be giving the candidate time to ask you some questions too.

Here are two examples of what different interviewers may say:

- 'I'm the office manager and if you were to be successful in getting this job, you would be working directly for me. I'd like to spend the next 45 minutes talking a little about your administrative skills. Towards the end of the interview, I'll give you time to ask any questions that you may have and finally I'll explain next steps.'
- 'As I mentioned, I'm Alex Henley and I'm the human resources manager here. You're going to be spending two hours here with us – the first hour will be spent with me. My job as a human resources manager is to ask you some broader questions about your general skills. After you and I are done, my colleague Chris Peterson, who is a business development manager, will be taking over and asking you some more specific, technical questions about the role. And Chris will be giving you time to ask questions about the role and to explain next steps should you be successful in this interview round.'

Explaining the interview approach

In introducing the concept of competency-based interviewing, you need to get across certain key points:

- Competency-based interviewing tries to look at the candidate's behaviours and skills in real situations that happened in the *past*.
- The candidate should try to focus on *specific* examples of situations as opposed to talking about how they *generally* deal with such situations.
- The candidate should try to come up with examples that are as recent as possible.

- As an interviewer, you are looking only for certain information. So if the candidate is not providing you with that information, you may interrupt occasionally and steer them with further questions.
- To aid your recall, you will be taking notes.

An example explanation about the concept and style of competency-based interviewing might be broken down as follows:

'This is going to be a competency-based interview. Have you been through a competency-based interview before? Competencies are essentially the skills and behaviours that are necessary to do the job. And in order to understand your skills, I'd like to explore how you have tackled some actual situations in the past. So rather than talking about how you might *hypothetically* tackle situations or how you *generally* tackle situations, I'd like you to think back to *specific* situations you have been in.

'If you could stick to situations within the last six months, that would be great. But ideally we would not go back more than a year or so. Not every example has to be from your work. For example, if you can think of a great project you worked on outside of your paid work, you can talk about that.

'I'm looking for specific evidence of how you have handled past situations. What a lot of candidates find is that they want to give me more information about the background and context. But actually I'm most interested in the actions you took and the results you achieved. So I will probably interrupt you occasionally if I've got enough information. Please don't be put off by that, as my interrupting you only means that I've heard whatever I needed from you.

'I'll be taking some notes to help me remember correctly what you said. So please don't be put off by that either.'

Explaining the interview approach in writing

Competency-based interviewing is not intended to be an underhand or secret technique. In fact, it works best when candidates understand fully what they are being asked for, ie to provide specific instances of past behaviour.

As such, some organisations actually put information about this style of interviewing on their websites or write to candidates before their interviews to outline the interview approach. Providing guidance for candidates ahead of time makes them feel more comfortable and allows you, the interviewer, to gain information more quickly.

If you want to help candidates understand what they are being asked to do, you could write to them or post on your website a couple of paragraphs along the lines of the following:

> At (name of organisation) we use a style of interviewing called competency-based interviewing. A competency is merely a skill or behaviour that we believe is essential for effective performance within the job. You should be able to figure out the key competencies that are required for the role based on the job advert.
>
> During the interview, you will be asked for examples of situations that you have experienced that are relevant to each skill. For example, you may be asked to talk about a project that you once managed, a team you were a part of, or a difficult customer you had to deal with.
>
> We are interested in hearing about actual examples of situations that you experienced. When describing these situations, help yourself to present your experience in the best possible light by following these pointers:
>
> - Listen carefully to the question and choose a relevant example from your experience. Ideally, the example should be from the last six months, but not older than a few years. You may choose to talk about examples either from your work or from outside of your work. Choose the example that you think best shows off your skills.
> - Give a short overview of the situation. Explain the context and how the situation arose.
> - Spend most of your time talking about the actions and decisions you took.
> - Finally, tell us about the results or outcomes that you achieved.

Before launching into your interview questions, make a final check that the candidate understands what you have explained. By this point, very few candidates will in practice have any questions. However, be ready to explain in a different way if a candidate has not understood fully the purpose and style of the interview.

Checking facts

The main bulk of the interview should consist of competency-based questions. However, should you need to check any facts about candidates' applications, the best time to do so is immediately after having introduced yourself and explained how you will run the interview. If there are any omissions or unclear areas on a candidate's CV or application, you may wish to ask some direct questions to clear these up immediately.

Consider, for example, whether you need to check any facts around qualifications or minimum standards of educational attainment, dates of employment, etc. Or you may need to see original documents such as certificates proving their qualifications, proof of eligibility to work and so on (because a significant proportion of candidates unfortunately do fake qualifications – especially if they can get away with bringing in photocopies rather than showing originals). If you discover that a candidate lied about his or her qualifications on an application form, you have the option of ending the interview immediately should the matter be sufficiently serious.

8

Competencies and example interview questions

The person specification that you created for the vacancy (see Chapter 2) should give you a strong prompt as to the competencies required of your ideal candidate. The principle of good interviewing is that you should aim to ask questions that cover the broad skills that have been identified in the person specification.

Having a set of competencies written down *before* you interview is useful because it gives you a guide against which to *evaluate the answers* you hear from candidates. Anyone can ask competency-based questions; the difficult part comes in evaluating the answers in a consistent and fair fashion. And that's where the lists of behaviours contained within each competency definition come into their own.

This chapter gives examples of a number of broad, generic competencies that you could use. Each section within this chapter defines the competency and outlines briefly the kinds of behaviour that you should be listening out for when candidates talk through their examples. Each section then gives examples of interview funnels that you may wish to use.

Instructions for using the competencies

The competencies contained within this chapter are *generic* competencies, ie they are written with no specific organisation in mind. You will therefore notice that each competency '*could* include' certain behaviours. However, the precise behaviours that each competency should include may vary according to factors such as:

- *The nature of the role.* For example, consider the competency of selling. A sales person who sells complex IT projects to corporate clients would need to sell in a different way from a sales person who cold-calls customers on the telephone to sell them tangible products.
- *The culture of the organisation.* For example, what an engineering business would define as thinking analytically might be very different from what an advertising firm defines as thinking analytically. Remember therefore that the competencies in this chapter are *generic* and ideally need tailoring for your organisation and the nature of each role.
- *The seniority of the role.* Consider that the level of performance you are looking for in a candidate for an entry-level role will necessarily be different from the level of capability you may need from a senior manager. As such, you should tailor not only the definitions of each competency but also adapt the interview funnels for your own use.

Bear in mind that it takes even experienced interviewers around 10 minutes to probe one competency in depth. As such, it is likely that you will have to select a small number of competencies against which to interview candidates rather than asking all candidates questions against all of the competencies in this chapter.

Furthermore, rather than simply picking a handful of competencies against which to interview, you should ideally work through the process of creating a job description and/or a person specification. For example, while planning and organising may be a big part of some roles, it may be irrelevant for others. Leading and inspiring others may only be important for management roles. And thinking and behaving commercially may only be important for roles in profit-focused organisations.

There is some overlap between the competencies. For example, some of the behaviours contained within the competencies 'influencing others', 'serving customers' and 'communicating with others' do have common characteristics. However, you should decide which of these competencies is most relevant not only to your organisation but to each specific role that you are interviewing for.

To sum up how to use the following competencies then: consider the competencies in this chapter as *generic*, *broad* competencies that are likely to need tailoring based on the precise nature of the role for which you are interviewing.

Thinking analytically

Definition of thinking analytically: 'Identifies information to analyse, and applies logical reasoning skills to come up with informed decisions.'

Thinking analytically *could* include the following behaviours:

- Breaks problems down into their essential parts.
- Identifies the information required for analysis.
- Identifies patterns and themes in data.
- Uses both quantitative and qualitative data for analysis.
- Demonstrates logical reasoning skills.
- Makes decisions and proposes solutions even when the data may be slightly ambiguous.

Thinking analytically – Example question funnel 1

1. **Situation** 'Describe a time you had to analyse a problem.'
   'When did this happen?'
   'How did this situation arise?'
2. **Task** 'What was the task you had to do?'
3. **Actions** 'What data did you gather?'
   'How did you go about analysing the data?'
   'What were your initial thoughts about the data?'
   'What themes or patterns emerged from the data?'
4. **Result** 'What were your recommendations?'
5. **Summarise (if necessary)** 'So if I understood you correctly, you…'

Thinking analytically – Example question funnel 2

1. **Situation** 'Tell me about the last time you had to analyse some data.'
   'When exactly did this happen?'
2. **Task** 'Why were you trying to analyse the data?'
3. **Actions** 'How did you go about analysing the data?'
   'Talk me through your thought process.'
   'What problems did you experience along the way?'
   'How did you deal with those problems?'
   'Who, if anyone, did you talk to or seek advice from?'
   'What else did you do in analysing the data?'
4. **Result** 'What were your ultimate findings?'
5. **Summarise (if necessary)** 'So to repeat back to you what you did, you…'

Planning and organising

Definition of planning and organising: 'Works out the series of actions and the resources required in order to achieve a goal.'

This competency *could* include the following behaviours:

- Manages own time.
- Breaks down complex goals into more manageable tasks.
- Decides on the timing of different tasks necessary to achieve an end goal.
- Considers what resources may be necessary.
- Creates contingency plans in case of problems.

Planning and organising – Example question funnel 1

1. **Situation**	'Tell me about a project (or assignment or a large piece of work) that you planned from the beginning.' 'When did this happen?'
2. **Task**	'How did you come to be managing this project?'
3. **Actions**	'How did you start planning and organising it?' 'What resources did you need to make the project happen?' 'Who, if anyone, did you need to involve in the planning?' 'What else did you do in creating the plan for the project?'
4. **Result**	'What feedback did you get about the success of the project?'
5. **Summarise (if necessary)**	'To recap briefly what happened, you...'

Planning and organising – Example question funnel 2

1. **Situation** 'Please tell me about any party or event you were in charge of planning and organising.'
   'How long ago did this happen?'
2. **Task** 'Tell me a little about how you came to be in charge of this.'
3. **Actions** 'How did you begin to tackle it?'
   'What problems did you experience along the way?'
   'How did you deal with those problems?'
   'What kinds of contingencies did you cover in creating the plan?'
4. **Result** 'How did the event go in the end?'
5. **Summarise (if necessary)** 'So to repeat back to you what you did, you...'

Demonstrating drive and determination

Definition of demonstrating drive and determination: 'Persists in the face of setbacks and obstacles and motivates self to achieve results and get things done.'

Demonstrating drive and determination *could* include the following behaviours:

- Prioritises actions (eg decides what can be done and what cannot) when time is short
- Finds ways to deal with problems and barriers
- Takes the initiative when appropriate
- Puts extra time/effort into work to ensure it gets done
- Seeks and obtains appropriate assistance from others to ensure the work gets done
- Completes tasks and assignments on time and within budget.

Demonstrating drive and determination – Example question funnel 1

1. **Situation**	'Tell me about a project or piece of work that did not go according to plan.' 'When exactly did this happen?'
2. **Task**	'What was your involvement in this situation?'
3. **Actions**	'How did you deal with those difficulties?' 'What else went wrong?' 'And how did you deal with that problem?' 'Whom, if anyone, did you need to involve to try to help you with the project?' 'What else did you do to get things back on track?'
4. **Result**	'What was the outcome of the project?'
5. **Summarise (if necessary)**	'If I understand you correctly, you...'

Demonstrating drive and determination – Example question funnel 2

1. **Situation**	'Tell me about a difficult project that you were in charge of managing to its completion.' 'When did this happen?'
2. **Task**	'How did you come to be in charge of it?' 'Why was it difficult?'
3. **Actions**	'What problems cropped up along the way?' 'How did you deal with that first problem?' 'How did you deal with that second problem?' 'How did you deal with that next problem?'
4. **Result**	'So what feedback did you get about the project in the end?'
5. **Summarise (if necessary)**	'To recap briefly, you...'

Serving customers

Definition of serving customers: 'Seeks to understand customer requirements and works to exceed them.'

Serving customers *could* include the following behaviours:

- Asks questions to understand customer needs.
- Reads customer body language to understand unspoken needs.
- Engages in customer interactions with enthusiasm.
- Puts customer needs ahead of other work.
- Looks for ways to exceed customers' expectations.

Serving customers – Example question funnel 1

1. **Situation** 'Describe for me a time you exceeded a customer's expectations.'
   'When did this happen?'
2. **Task** 'What was your involvement?'
3. **Actions** 'How did you establish the customer's needs?'
   'How did you respond to those needs?'
   'In what way did you exceed the customer's expectations?'
   'How did the customer respond to what you did?'
4. **Result** 'How did you know that you had exceeded – and not just met – the customer's needs?'
5. **Summarise (if necessary)** 'It sounds to me as if you...'

Serving customers – Example question funnel 2

1. **Situation** 'Tell me about a difficult customer you dealt with.'
   'When did you deal with this particular customer?'
2. **Task** 'In what way was the customer being difficult?'
3. **Actions** 'What questions did you ask to establish the customer's problem?

		'What options did you consider for dealing with the customer?' 'What steps did you take to deal with the situation?' 'How did the customer respond to what you did?'
4.	**Result**	'How did the situation resolve itself in the end?'
5.	**Summarise (if necessary)**	'To sum up then, you...'

Working in a team

Definition of working in a team: 'Actively participates as a part of the team, providing support as necessary to ensure the achievement of team goals.'

Working in a team *could* include the following behaviours:

- Proactively checks whether other members of the team need assistance.
- Offers emotional support and/or practical assistance as appropriate to members of the team.
- Shares information and ideas with other members of the team.
- Tackles any sources of conflict or poor communication within the team.
- Adapts own role within the team as required.
- Shares credit and offers praise to others.

Working in a team – Example question funnel 1

1.	**Situation**	'Tell me about a time when you made a significant contribution to a team goal.' 'How long ago did this happen?'

2. **Task** 'What was the team trying to achieve at the time?'
'What was your contribution?'
3. **Actions** 'Talk me through *exactly* what you said or did to contribute to the team.'
'What impact did your contribution have on the overall team?'
4. **Result** 'How did the team do in terms of trying to reach the goal?'
5. **Summarise (if necessary)** 'To recap what I'm hearing, you...'

Working in a team – Example question funnel 2

1. **Situation** 'Tell me about a time when you were instrumental in helping out a colleague.'
'How long ago did this happen?'
2. **Task** 'Why did this person need helping out?'
3. **Actions** 'What did you do or say to help your colleague?'
'How did your colleague respond to your efforts?'
'What else did you try to do?' (repeat this question as necessary)
4. **Result** 'What was the eventual outcome of all of this?'
5. **Summarise (if necessary)** 'It sounds to me as if you...'

Learning and developing oneself

Definition of learning and developing oneself: 'Actively seeks feedback from others and opportunities to improve.'

Learning and developing oneself *could* include the following behaviours:

- Seeks feedback and constructive criticism from others.
- Identifies and pursues opportunities to learn
- Learns in a variety of ways, eg from reading, shadowing others, discussion, etc.
- Analyses the lessons from mistakes.
- Changes own behaviour in the light of learning.

Learning and developing oneself – Example question funnel 1

1. **Situation**	'Tell me about the last activity you undertook to develop yourself.' 'When was this?'
2. **Task**	'What were you trying to achieve?'
3. **Actions**	'What activities did you undertake exactly?' 'Who else, if anyone, did you involve in trying to develop yourself?' 'Describe the problems or difficulties you encountered along the way in trying to develop yourself.' 'How did you overcome those difficulties?'
4. **Result**	'What have you learnt?'
5. **Summarise (if necessary)**	'In summary then, you...'

Learning and developing oneself – Example question funnel 2

1. **Situation**	'Tell me about the last time you were criticised.' 'When did this happen?'
2. **Task**	'Please tell me precisely what that person said.'
3. **Actions**	'How did you respond to what was said?' 'What did you do about the criticism?' 'What else did you do?'
4. **Result**	'Tell me how that incident has changed your behaviour.'
5. **Summarise (if necessary)**	'In summary then, you...'

Influencing others

Definition of influencing others: 'Winning others over to a new point of view, by using either logical arguments or other persuasive tactics.'

Influencing others *could* include the following behaviours:

- Identifies the key people to influence.
- Asks questions to understand the needs and wants of those to be influenced.
- Identifies unspoken agendas.
- Adapts personal style to meet the needs of different situations.
- Leaves the other parties feeling positive about the outcome.
- Ensures that the ensuing decisions and outcomes align to organisational objectives.

Influencing others – Example question funnel 1

1. **Situation**	'Talk me through an occasion when you had to change someone's mind.' 'When did this happen?'
2. **Task**	'Why were you trying to change that person's mind?' 'What was that person's initial stance?'
3. **Actions**	'What did you try to do?' 'Exactly what did you do or say?' 'How did that person respond?' 'Talk me through what else you tried and how that person responded.'
4. **Result**	'What was the end result?'
5. **Summarise (if necessary)**	'If I understand correctly, you…'

Influencing others – Example question funnel 2

1. **Situation**	'Describe a situation in which you dealt with someone you did not originally see eye-to-eye with.' 'How long ago was this?' 'What was the other person's point of view?'
2. **Task**	'What options did you consider in tackling this situation?'
3. **Actions**	'Describe your approach in trying to influence them to your point of view.' 'How did that person respond?' 'What else did you do or say to bring them round to your point of view?'
4. **Result**	'What happened in the end?'
5. **Summarise (if necessary)**	'To recap, you...'

Thinking and behaving commercially

Definition of thinking and behaving commercially: 'Appreciates the need to manage budgets and costs in the pursuit of greater efficiency and/or profitability.'

Thinking and behaving commercially *could* include the following behaviours:

- Demonstrates sensitivity to costs and wastage.
- Spots opportunities for reducing costs and/or increasing revenues.
- Uses financial analyses as appropriate.
- Makes cutbacks and adjustments as necessary to balance a budget.
- Is aware of the pros and cons of different choices.

Thinking and behaving commercially – Example question funnel 1

1. **Situation** 'Tell me about a commercially difficult project that you were involved in.'
   'When did this take place?'
2. **Task** 'What were the financial or commercial goals of the project?'
   'Why did the situation become difficult?'
   'What was your role in the project?'
3. **Actions** 'How did you try to contribute to the commercial or financial aspects of the project?'
   'What options did you consider?'
   'What did you do to tackle those difficulties?'
   'What else did you do?'
4. **Result** 'What happened in the end?'
5. **Summarise (if necessary)** 'To summarise then, you...'

Thinking and behaving commercially – Example question funnel 2

1. **Situation** 'Tell me about a difficult financial decision you had to make.'
   'How long ago was this?'
2. **Task** 'What was your involvement with the decision?'
   'Why was it a difficult decision?'
3. **Actions** 'What analyses did you do to help you make your decision?'
   'What options did you consider?'
   'What were the pros and cons of each option?'
   'What option did you go for in the end?'
4. **Result** 'What was the impact of your decision?'
5. **Summarise (if necessary)** 'To sum up what I seem to be hearing, you...'

Communicating with others

Definition of communicating with others: 'Produces clear and effective communication, both in writing and verbally, both in formal and in informal situations.'

Communicating with others *could* include the following behaviours:

- Writes documents that get across key points in a clear and concise fashion.
- Speaks up and puts own opinions forward, eg in team or customer meetings.
- Adapts approach (eg knows when to speak to someone one-on-one as opposed to in a group) depending on the needs of the audience.
- Puts together and delivers effective formal presentations.
- Seeks feedback to confirm the effectiveness of own communications.

Communicating with others – Example question funnel 1

1. **Situation**	'Describe a situation in which you had to communicate a difficult message to either an individual or a group.' 'When did this happen?'
2. **Task**	'What was the message you needed to communicate?' 'Why was this a difficult message to communicate?'
3. **Actions**	'What options did you have in getting across your message?' 'What approach did you settle on to convey the message?' 'Why did you choose that approach?' 'How did your audience respond to your message?' 'What else did you do?'

4. **Result** 'What feedback did you receive about the success of your communication?'
5. **Summarise (if necessary)** 'To summarise then, you…'

Communicating with others – Example question funnel 2

1. **Situation** 'Tell me about a time when you had to get a complex point across in a short space of time.' 'How long ago did this take place?'
2. **Task** 'What were you trying to get across?' 'Why was this a complex point to get across?'
3. **Actions** 'How did you begin to tackle the situation?' 'What tactic did you choose for conveying your message?' 'What else did you do?'
4. **Result** 'How did you know you had succeeded in getting your point across?'
5. **Summarise (if necessary)** 'If I understand correctly, you…'

Building relationships

Definition of building relationships: 'Establishes rapport, seeks to understand the wants and needs of others, and treats others with respect.'

Building relationships *could* include the following behaviours:

- Approaches other people with enthusiasm (as opposed to waiting for others to approach oneself).
- Asks questions to establish wants and needs of others.
- Recognises different perspectives (eg cultural, national, organisational, and other differences).
- Seeks to establish common ground.
- Treats others with respect.

Building relationships – Example question funnel 1

1. **Situation** 'Talk me through an occasion in which you built a relationship with someone.'
   'When did this take place?'
2. **Task** 'Why were you interacting with this person to begin with?'
3. **Actions** 'How did you begin to build the relationship?'
   'Talk me through all of the steps you took in building the relationship.'
   'What difficulties did you encounter?'
   'What did you do to overcome those difficulties?'
4. **Result** 'What happened in the end?'
5. **Summarise (if necessary)** 'To recap then, you…'

Building relationships – Example question funnel 2

1. **Situation** 'Tell me about the most difficult colleague you have had to deal with.'
   'When did this happen?'
2. **Task** 'Why did you need to build a relationship with this colleague?'
3. **Actions** 'What approach did you take to build the relationship?'
   'Tell me what else you did to build the relationship.'
   'How did your colleague respond to your attempts to build the relationship?'
   'What did you find most difficult to deal with?'
   'How did you overcome those difficulties?'
4. **Result** 'What kind of a relationship did you manage to build in the end?'
5. **Summarise (if necessary)** 'So it sounds to me as if you…'

Managing change

Managing change is defined as: 'Demonstrates a positive approach to the challenge of change and not only looks for ways to make change happen but also to encourage and support others through change too.'

Managing change *could* include behaviours such as:

- Adapts positively (rather than grudgingly) to changing circumstances.
- Asks questions that challenge assumptions and the established status quo.
- Actively seeks out opportunities to change systems, processes, or ways of working for the benefit of the organisation.
- Approaches change with enthusiasm (rather than opposing it).
- Encourages and supports others in making change happen.

Managing change – Example question funnel 1

1. **Situation**	'Describe a recent occasion in which you changed some way of working within your team or organisation.' 'When did this happen?'
2. **Task**	'Why did you think it needed changing?' 'Who did you need to involve to make the change happen?'
3. **Actions**	'What did you do to bring about the change?' 'What problems or barriers did you encounter in trying to bring about the change?' 'How did you overcome those barriers?' 'What other actions did you take to make the change successful?'
4. **Result**	'What was the result you achieved?'
5. **Summarise (if necessary)**	'To summarise then, you...'

Managing change – Example question funnel 2

1. **Situation** 'Give me an example of a situation in which you saw an opportunity to improve an ineffective practice or way of working.'
'When did this happen?'
2. **Task** 'How did you spot the opportunity?'
3. **Actions** 'How did you go about tackling the opportunity?'
'Taking me back to the beginning, talk me through each individual step you took to make the improvement.'
'What were the toughest parts about making the improvement a reality?'
'What else did you do?'
4. **Result** 'What was the outcome of your efforts?'
5. **Summarise (if necessary)** 'To recap, you…'

Selling

Selling is defined as: 'Builds relationships with new customers (or clients) and looks for ways to deepen relationships with existing customers (or clients) to sell them products or services.'

Selling *could* include behaviours such as:

- Seeks and obtains opportunities to meet with new customers (eg through networking, cold-calling, marketing, or other activities as appropriate).
- Adapts personal style to match the style of different customers.
- Shows empathy for the needs of customers.
- Negotiates new business at profitable rates.
- Ensures that customers are happy with their purchases and looks for ways to gain new business (eg by maintaining the relationship or asking for referrals).

Selling – Example question funnel 1

1. **Situation**	'Tell me about a time you persuaded a customer or client to buy from you.' 'When was this?'
2. **Task**	'How did you come to know of the customer?'
3. **Actions**	'How did you go about discovering the customer's wants and needs?' 'What were the customer's concerns and needs?' 'What did you do to deal with those concerns and needs?' 'How did the individual respond to your efforts?' 'What tactics did you use to negotiate a good deal for your organisation?'
4. **Result**	'How much did you manage to sell in the end?'
5. **Summarise (if necessary)**	'To summarise then, you...'

Selling – Example question funnel 2

1. **Situation**	'Describe a customer situation where you worked hard but ultimately failed to win the customer's business.' 'When did this happen?'
2. **Task**	'How did you come to meet the customer?' 'Why did the customer not buy in the end?'
3. **Actions**	'Describe the tactics you tried to win the customer.' 'How did the customer respond to your efforts?' 'What else did you try?'
4. **Result**	'What did you learn from that customer?'
5. **Summarise (if necessary)**	'To summarise then, you...'

Leading and inspiring others

Leading and inspiring others is defined as: 'Provides clear instruction to members of the team and encourages, inspires, and develops them.'

Leading and inspiring others *could* include behaviours such as:

- Consults members of the team in drawing up plans.
- Conveys a clear sense of direction to members of the team
- Delegates work effectively.
- Conveys a sense of trust in others.
- Builds confidence in others through coaching, encouragement and praise.
- Tackles underperformance by providing accurate and timely feedback.

Leading and inspiring others – Example question funnel 1

1. **Situation**	'Give me an example of a recent occasion you coached one of the members of your team.' 'When did this happen?'
2. **Task**	'Why did you decide to coach that person?'
3. **Actions**	'How did you first broach the issue with the individual?' 'Starting from your initial discussion, talk me through the steps you took.' 'How did the individual respond to your efforts?' 'How else did you coach and develop this person?'
4. **Confirm**	'What has since happened to that person?'
5. **Summarise (if necessary)**	'To summarise then, you...'

Leading and inspiring others – Example question funnel 2

1. **Situation**	'Tell me about a time you had to motivate your team.' 'When did this happen?' 'Briefly, tell me about your team so I can understand the background.'
2. **Task**	'Why did they need motivating?'
3. **Actions**	'How did you tackle the task of motivating them?' 'What steps did you take to motivate the team?' 'How did the team respond to your early efforts?' 'What else did you do to motivate them?'
4. **Result**	'What evidence did you have to know that you had succeeded in motivating them?'
5. **Summarise (if necessary)**	'If I understand what you've been saying correctly, you...'

Further competencies

Remember that the sample competencies contained in this chapter are only *generic* competencies. The behaviours (and therefore competencies) that are expected in an insurance firm may not be relevant in a manufacturing business or an IT consultancy. As such, different organisations design their own competencies. Other competencies could include skills such as behaving ethically, coaching people, acting entrepreneurially, managing risk, innovating and thinking creatively, and so on.

Sample organisational competencies

There are literally hundreds of possible combinations of competencies. For example, Tables 8.1 and 8.2 give examples

Table 8.1 Competency set 1: A law firm

Technical knowledge
Communication
Commitment to delivering results
Teamworking
Leading and developing people
Managing budgets and finance
Managing quality
Caring for clients
Selling to clients

Table 8.2 Competency set 2: A bank

Creating vision
Acting strategically
Driving change
Judgement and decision making
Thinking commercially and entrepreneurially
Inspiring trust
Developing others
Winning new customers
Listening to others
Influencing people
Sharing knowledge
Flexibility and adaptability

of the competencies used by two different organisations that I have worked with.

Both organisations have a large number of competencies. However, not all of the competencies are relevant to all roles. For example, candidates for roles as junior lawyers at the law firm (see Table 8.1) would be interviewed against the competencies of technical knowledge, communication, commitment to delivering results, and teamworking. Only candidates for the more senior legal positions that are responsible for managing clients are interviewed against the competencies of leading and developing people, managing budgets and finance, managing quality, and selling to clients.

Tailoring and creating your own competencies

Different organisations like to use different names for their competencies. What one organisation may call 'commercial thinking', another organisation may call 'commercial and business acumen', and a third organisation 'business awareness'. The names of the competencies matter less than how they are defined and the behaviours you would expect a candidate at that level to be able to demonstrate.

In creating competencies (and therefore questions) for your own organisation, bear in mind the following pointers:

- A competency should aim to measure only observable behaviour. Unless a competency tries to capture the behaviours that successful people say they use, your competency will not be able to distinguish between strong and weak candidates.
- The behaviours should be ones that your colleagues agree are associated with successful performance on the job.
- Each behaviour should include a verb phrase. In other words, it should describe an action that you can listen out for during the interview.
- A good competency should capture at least four or more behaviours.
- The behaviours you would expect of a junior member of the team are likely to differ from those you would expect of a more senior member of the team. Therefore many organisations have different competencies for junior, middle and senior employees within the organisation.

One of the most important points about designing a set of competencies is that what works for other organisations is unlikely to work for you. As an example, consider Table 8.3,

Table 8.3 Two organisations' versions of the 'serving customers' competency

Serving customers (for retailer)	Serving customers (for IT consultancy)
Definition of serving customers: 'Seeks to understand customer requirements and works to exceed them.'	Definition of serving customers: 'Builds long-term and profitable relationships with customers.'
Serving customers includes the following behaviours:	Serving customers includes the following behaviours:
■ Ask questions to understand customer needs ■ Reads customers' body language to understand unspoken needs ■ Engages in customer interactions with enthusiasm ■ Puts customer needs ahead of other work ■ Looks for ways to exceed customers' expectations	■ Adapts personal style to build relationships with customers ■ Collaborates with customers to understand their business needs ■ Negotiates deals with customers that balance customer profitability with the costs of meeting customer needs ■ Oversees other departments to ensure our organisation delivers projects that meet customers' expectations

which sets out two versions of the competency, 'serving customers'. The version on the left may be more appropriate for a retail organisation in which sales consultants are dealing with customers on a shop floor; the version on the right may be more appropriate for an organisation in which sales people try to sell complex pieces of specially designed IT equipment to corporate customers.

Remember therefore that the competencies contained within this chapter are generic competencies. To be of most use for your organisation, you need to think about the particular nature of each vacancy that you are trying to fill.

Technical knowledge

Certain jobs (eg computer programmers, lawyers, scientific researchers) may require specific technical knowledge. It is outside of the remit of this book to provide endless lists of possible questions. However, consider the following pointers in designing your technical competencies and interview questions:

- Decide on the knowledge that a candidate at any particular level should have. In particular, candidates for a junior role will likely need to have less knowledge than candidates being considered for a senior role.
- Discuss, if you can, with your colleagues whether the knowledge requirement is right for candidates at this level. Rather than rely only on your own thoughts on the requirements for a particular role, it is always better to get the opinions of knowledgeable colleagues to ensure that the requirements are neither too harsh nor too simple.
- Put together a list of the behaviours that the candidate should therefore be able to demonstrate (see Tables 8.4 and 8.5 for examples).
- Insist that all interviewers ask only questions relating to those specific behaviours, to ensure they do not treat some candidates more leniently than others.

Table 8.4 Sample technical competency for an entry-level programmer

Definition of technical knowledge: 'Has a basic understanding of key concepts related to programming.'

Technical knowledge includes behaviours such as:

- Explains when to use an assembler as opposed to a high-level programming language
- Understands how to use a debugger
- Understands when to use an emulator
- Can use a compiler

Table 8.5 Sample technical competency for a human resources manager

---

Definition of technical human resources skill: 'Has a deep understanding of how to apply human resources policies and procedures to assist line managers in delivering organisational goals.'

Technical human resources skill includes behaviours such as:

- Able to administer a compensation and benefits programme
- Able to manage recruitment and selection programmes
- Uses performance management techniques to enhance employee performance and deal with poor performers
- Demonstrates an understanding of relevant legal frameworks in hiring and firing employees
- Delivers training and development programmes.

As a further example, consider the person specification for the marketing director role from Chapter 2 contained within Table 2.2. While the marketing director might be expected to demonstrate broad competencies such as 'leading and inspiring others' and 'thinking and behaving commercially', it might also be reasonable to expect the ideal candidate to be able to demonstrate specific technical knowledge around marketing, which might include behaviours such as:

- conducting customer research;
- developing pricing policies;
- working with the sales team to achieve sales and profit targets;
- and so on.

What technical competencies might be relevant to the vacancies that you are trying to fill within your organisation?

9

Discussing money

Most of us need to work for a living and many of us are attracted to new jobs at least in part because they can pay us more money. However, it is one of the great pretences for interview candidates to say that they are not interested in the money. Most of the advice aimed at candidates tells them not to bring up the money issue. In fact, candidates are often told to deflect discussions about salary and benefits until they have been offered the job and persuaded the interviewers that they are the best qualified for the job.

Savvy candidates will do everything they can to avoid answering direct questions about pay and benefits. Discussions about money have often been likened to games of poker: whoever mentions a concrete figure first loses.

Questions about money

The following represents a list of questions that you could *possibly* ask. However, some may be more appropriate than others. For example, if you wish to be fairly direct about asking about someone's salary, try questions such as:

- 'Taking all of your bonuses into account, what are you earning at the moment?'

- 'What kind of salary are you looking for?'
- 'Please review your salary history for me – how much did you earn in your previous job? How much are you earning in your current job?'

If you wish to take a more indirect approach to discussing salary, try questions such as:

- 'What kind of salary progression would you expect in this role?'
- 'I understand your reluctance to commit to the precise salary you'd want to work for. But can you give me a range so I can understand if we can afford you?'
- 'We are offering a salary of X to Y. Would you be willing to work for a salary within this range?'

Do not forget that many candidates' overall pay packages can be made up of various guaranteed and performance-related bonuses. In order to investigate these, try questions such as:

- 'How is your total package made up?'
- 'How much does overtime contribute to your overall earnings?'
- 'What proportion of your total earnings is made up by sales commission?'
- 'Could you talk me through any bonuses you typically earn?'
- 'How much bonus did you receive last year?'
- 'What options do you currently have?'
- 'How much does your current employer contribute to your pension?'
- 'What non-cash benefits do you currently receive?'

Bear in mind that some of these questions may be more appropriate in the later stages of the interview process than others. In the first stage of the interview, you should be satisfied that there is sufficient match between the range that you are willing to pay and the range that the candidate might be willing to accept.

You should only ask questions about the detail of a candidate's package (eg about pensions and non-cash benefits) when you have decided to make an offer to a particular candidate and wish to negotiate exactly how much to pay him or her.

Persisting on the money issue

Candidates are so well schooled in deflecting questions about money that novice interviewers may experience exchanges not dissimilar to the following:

I: 'What kind of salary are you looking for?'
C: 'The most important factor for me is to find a job that will challenge me and help me to grow, so I'd rather not talk about money at the moment.'
I: 'Oh, OK.'

If you ask questions about money in the early rounds of the interview, you may find smart candidates saying that they are more interested in finding a challenging position, an organisation with a great reputation, opportunities to learn and grow, the right company culture, and so on. However, you should persist gently. After all, you need to know whether you can afford to pay the candidate. If the top salary you are able to pay is less than what they are looking for, there's little point continuing with the interview process.

Consider the following example between a candidate who is reluctant to discuss money and a tenacious interviewer who needs to understand whether the organisation can afford the candidate:

I: 'What kind of salary are you looking for?'
C: 'The most important factor for me is to find a job that will challenge me and help me to grow, so I'd rather not talk about money at the moment.'

I: 'I can understand your reluctance to talk about money, but I need to establish that we can afford you. Could you tell me how much you are earning at the moment?'

C: 'What I'm earning at the moment doesn't really matter as I really am looking for a role that will stretch me.'

I: 'I appreciate that you are looking for the right role. But I hope you can understand that I must persist with this line of questioning until you give me an answer. Once you've answered this one question, we can move on: What is your current package at the moment?'

C: '£60,000 plus a performance-related bonus that worked out at around 20 per cent last year. Plus a 5 per cent pension contribution and health insurance.'

I: 'Thank you. Let's move on...'

In the example, you can see that the interviewer begins with a very simple question. It is only when the candidate deliberately avoids giving a straight answer that the interviewer is forced to resort to a more direct line of questioning.

So long as you *keep your tone and manner light and friendly*, you will find that the majority of candidates will eventually give you an answer. However, do remember to monitor your behaviour and tone of voice. When interviewing strong candidates, remember that the candidates are deciding whether they want to work for your organisation as much as you are evaluating their likely fit with your organisation and the job.

Wrapping up the interview

Notice periods and non-compete clauses

You may wish to ask a final question to establish the candidate's notice period. Employees working in relatively junior positions may have notice periods of only a few weeks; senior managers often have notice periods of several months.

If a candidate is not currently working, you may still need to find out when the candidate would be able to start work. Do not assume that candidates who are not working would be able to start immediately – they may have family commitments or holidays booked in. If you are interviewing more senior candidates, you may also wish to ask about clauses in their contract with their current or most recent employers that may prohibit them from working for a competitor or bringing customers or clients with them too.

Answering candidates' questions

It is traditional to allow some time towards the end of the interview to answer candidates' questions. If there is only one interview before you decide whom to appoint, you need to make sure that candidates have a realistic understanding of the job you may be about to offer them. You want to avoid offering a candidate the job only for him or her to discover that the job is not what was expected and to quit. Imagine having to go through all the hassle and expense of recruiting someone new all over again. As such, you should be ready to talk about the conditions of employment, the nature of the role, and what it is like to work for the organisation.

Some interviewers believe that they can tell a lot about a candidate by the questions that are asked. For example, these interviewers believe that a candidate who asks about the salary is driven only by money; or that a candidate who asks about the length of the working day is likely to be poorly motivated and willing to work only the minimum hours required. However, it is dangerous to make such assumptions as such guesses about candidates' motives can be (and frequently are) wrong. Avoid judging candidates based on their questions and instead allow them to ask you questions purely for them to gather information on the role and your organisation.

Scheduling time for questions

Be sure to plan into your interview schedule sufficient time to answer candidates' questions. The number and type of questions you may get asked depend on a variety of factors. Some rules of thumb:

- Consider the amount of information you have already provided. If your organisation has provided information about the role, the team and the organisation perhaps on your website or in a recruitment brochure, you would reasonably expect candidates to have fewer questions. On the other hand, if you have hired an executive search firm to headhunt candidates in secret to lead a planned but as yet unannounced project, you should be prepared to answer many more questions.

- Allow more time for candidates to ask questions for senior and/or complex roles. If, for example, you are looking to hire a personal assistant, the role is likely to be more straightforward and well defined than that of a global head of technology.
- Allow more time for questions from candidates in later interview rounds. The balance of power shifts as the interview process progresses – away from the interviewer and towards candidates. Typically, the purpose of the first round of interviews is primarily for you as an interviewer to screen out unsuitable candidates. However, as you reduce the number of candidates over successive rounds, candidates increasingly need to think about whether they want to work for your organisation. As such, you should allow more time for candidates to learn more about the organisation and role during later interview rounds.

Likely questions

You should be ready to answer questions about the role, the nature of the work, and why the vacancy has arisen at this time. No list could ever be comprehensive, but you should be ready to answer questions such as:

- 'Why has this position become open?'
- 'What happened to the person who previously held the position?'
- 'What are the career prospects in this role?'
- 'If I were to be successful in getting the job and performed well in it, what could I reasonably be doing as a next move within the organisation?'
- 'When was the last person promoted?'
- 'What would my first project or assignment be?'

- 'What would my duties and responsibilities be?'
- 'What are the most significant tasks that you need completed by whoever gets this role within the next 12 months?'
- 'How would my performance be evaluated?'
- 'How often would my performance be evaluated?'
- 'What are the working hours generally like?'
- 'How much overtime do you foresee might be necessary on the job?'
- 'Could you tell me a bit more about the people that I'd be working with most closely?'

Culture is 'the way things get done' or the implicit rules that govern how people behave towards each other and go about their work. Smart candidates know that *how* people behave in dealing with each other and getting work done is often as important as *what* work gets done. Again, no list of questions can be totally comprehensive, but you should be ready to answer candidates' questions on aspects of the culture. Consider questions such as:

- 'How would you describe the culture of the organisation?'
- 'What do you most enjoy about working here?'
- 'What frustrations do people have about working here?'
- 'How much politicking and lobbying goes on within the organisation?'
- 'How much formality is there in the way people deal with each other here?'
- 'Generally speaking, what does it take to get promoted here?'
- 'Why do people fail to get on here?'
- 'Why do people decide to quit or get pushed from the organisation?'

Candidates may reasonably have questions about the structure, reputation and management of the organisation too. Be ready to answer questions such as:

- 'To whom would I report?'
- 'Could you tell me a bit more about the person who would be my line manager?'
- 'How much supervision would I get as a new employee?'
- 'What kind of training or induction would I receive on joining the organisation?'
- 'How many people would I be in charge of? What are they like?'
- 'What can you tell me about the organisation's strategy and growth plans?'
- 'What new products, services or initiatives are being planned that might affect me and this department?'
- 'How is the department that I'd be working for viewed by the rest of the organisation?'
- 'Could you talk me through the relevant parts of the organisation's structure?'
- 'If you were to offer me the job, could I meet some of the team before deciding whether to take the job or not?'

Selling the job

Remember that the interview process is as much about helping candidates to decide whether they would want to work for you as for you to decide who to offer jobs to. Just because you rate a candidate does not mean that he or she would automatically want to work for you.

In answering questions that candidates may have, interviewers vary in the extent to which they try to sell their organisation and play up the desirability of the role. Some interviewers play the role of the ambassador, trying to be very positive about the organisation and the job in an attempt to snare the best candidates. However, that approach can backfire – if you sell a role and the organisation too much, you risk over-promising and under-delivering. On the other hand, if you are too negative about the role and the organisation – perhaps in the belief that it is better to be honest about all of the difficulties associated with the work – you could inadvertently scare good candidates away from accepting any offer you may make.

You must ultimately decide for yourself how to represent your organisation. Broadly speaking, the more information you can give to candidates, the more self-selection by candidates there will be. Being candid about the downsides of the job may lose you a few candidates in the short run. But that may arguably be better than making unrealistic promises about the job, having a candidate join your organisation only to quit several months or even mere weeks later, and then having to go through the whole recruitment and selection process again.

Explaining next steps

Before bringing the interview to a close, you need to tell the candidate what will happen after the interview. Consider points such as:

- when the candidate might reasonably expect to hear from you and/or the other people involved in making the decision;
- how you will be getting in touch (eg telephoning or writing directly to the candidate versus telling a recruitment agency to relay a message back to the candidate);
- how many other candidates you have still yet to see;
- what the next stage or round of the interview process might look like (if there is one);
- (if appropriate) how the candidate will be reimbursed for travel expenses.

Finally, remember to thank the candidate warmly for their time in coming to attend the interview.

Making spontaneous offers

Be extremely careful about making spontaneous offers. If you have yet to see all of the candidates, you risk making an offer and then meeting an even better candidate. Bear in mind that an offer of employment need not be in writing to constitute a legally binding contract.

Only make a spontaneous offer if: (i) you have seen all of the other candidates, (ii) you are completely certain that this candidate is very definitely stronger than the other candidates that you have already seen, and (iii) you feel that making an immediate offer will make a critical difference in securing this highly talented person.

The safer alternative to making a spontaneous offer is to wait until you have again read through the notes you took during the interview and rated the candidate to allow you to compare this candidate to the others you have seen (see Chapter 11). There is rarely anything to lose by waiting an extra half an hour to evaluate properly the notes you took on the candidate and ringing him or her on the way home to make an offer.

11

Rating candidates and making a decision

Your main aim during an interview is to collect evidence about a candidate's past performance against your organisation's set of competencies. Having collected that evidence, the next step is to rate each candidate against those competencies so that you can compare the different candidates against each other as objectively as possible.

Once the interviews have ended, some interviewers try to compare the candidates against each other. However, this is not the best way to come to a decision about the ideal candidate; the most effective way is *first* to rate each candidate individually against the competencies and *only then* to compare candidates' scores against each other.

In order to rate candidates, you need to have a *marking frame* – a document that has three parts:

- a set of marking guidelines;
- a list of the behaviours for each competency;
- a rating scale.

Marking guidelines

Marking guidelines are simply a set of notes that help to remind you how to mark the interview. In general, the key steps to marking an interview are to:

- Wait until the interview has ended.
- Read through all of the notes you have taken. A handy tip is to underline or highlight key phrases (in particular, actions and decisions that the candidate told you about) in your notes using a coloured marker pen to help them stand out.
- Read the first competency and compare the evidence within your notes to the behaviours written down in the competency.
- Summarise the evidence from your notes by writing them up on the interview evaluation form.
- Rate the candidate on the rating scale.
- Repeat this process for the next competency until all of the competencies have been covered.

When rating candidates, aim to distinguish between content and delivery. Rate the examples the candidate gave you (ie *what* he or she said) rather than his or her demeanour (ie *how* he or she said it). Most untrained interviewers fall into the trap of rating delivery rather than content. Do not automatically mark down a candidate for nervousness or poor eye contact – just because someone is nervous during an interview does not necessarily mean that he or she will be nervous in front of customers or colleagues. Conversely, do not assume that someone who comes across as charming and likeable during an interview will necessarily display those same qualities in their day-to-day work.

Remember that your ratings of candidates must always be based on *evidence*. Ideally, you should only rate candidates based on what the candidate reported (and you wrote down) during the interview. Avoid relying on your instincts or mere 'suspicions'.

Behaviours and rating scale

The marking frame should also set out the behaviours that are related to a particular competency and invite the interviewer to tick them if a candidate talked about those behaviours in the interview. To help you compare candidates, you also need to rate each candidate on some kind of numerical rating scale. Bear in mind that a rating scale with only three ratings (eg 1 is 'poor', 2 is 'good' and 3 is 'outstanding') may not give you enough room to distinguish between candidates. On the other hand, having a rating scale with more than nine ratings may mean that it is difficult to differentiate meaningfully between any two adjacent ratings. In practice, most organisations have rating scales that are around five or seven points.

You can decide on whatever labels you wish to attach to the numbers on the rating scale. Figure 11.1 provides an example of three sets of rating scales to give you an idea of the kind of language that is commonly used to describe the numbers on rating scales.

Sample marking frame

On pages 130 to 133 is a sample marking frame for a job in which the organisation has decided that three competencies are of particular importance. Please note that this organisation has tailored its competencies, so these are slightly different from the generic competencies in Chapter 8.

1	2	3	4	5
Significant development needs	Minor development needs	Expected behaviour for someone at this level	Minor strengths	Significant strengths

7	Outstanding
6	Significant strengths
5	Some strengths
4	Competent
3	Some weaknesses
2	Significant weaknesses
1	Unacceptable

1	2	3	4	5
Considerably below par performance	Slightly below par performance	On par performance	Slightly above par performance	Considerably above par performance

Figure 11.1 Examples of three different rating scales

Marking frame page 1 of 4

This marking frame is designed to be used *after* you have finished your interview. Instructions are as follows:

- Start by writing on this page the candidate's name, interviewer(s)' name(s), and date that the interview took place.
- Read through your entire set of interview notes. Evidence against a particular competency could have been discussed at any point in the interview and not necessarily in answer to the 'right' question. It is therefore important to ensure that all of your notes are checked against all of the competencies.
- Start with the first competency and read through the list of behaviours. Tick any of the behaviours when you find evidence that the candidate demonstrated that behaviour in your notes.
- Put a cross against any of the behaviours when you find evidence that the candidate displayed the opposite of a behaviour.
- When there was no evidence that a candidate either demonstrated or did not demonstrate a behaviour, please leave the corresponding box blank.
- In the space provided, write a short summary of the evidence you collected for each competency.
- Finally, please staple or otherwise attach your handwritten notes to the back of this marking frame so that they may be kept together by human resources.

Candidate's name: ______________________________

Interviewer(s)' name(s): ______________________________

Date of interview: ______________________________

Marking frame page 2 of 4

DRIVE AND DETERMINATION

	Tick, cross or blank*
■ Prioritises tasks and activities	
■ Finds ways to deal with problems and barriers	
■ Goes the extra mile to get work done	
■ Asks for help from others when a work task is unclear	
■ Looks for ways to take on further responsibilities	

*Tick if behaviour was demonstrated; cross if opposite of behaviour was demonstrated; leave blank if neither

Summary of evidence:

____

____

____

____

____

Rating scale

Circle the rating that you give this candidate:

1	2	3	4	5
Weak performance, ie candidate displays 20 per cent or less of the behaviours	Some development needs, ie candidate displays only 30 to 40 per cent of behaviours	Moderate performance, ie candidate displays some 50 to 60 per cent of the behaviours	Strong performance, ie candidate displays most (80 per cent) of the listed behaviours	Exceptional performance, ie strong evidence that the candidate displayed all of the behaviours

Marking frame page 3 of 4

CUSTOMER SERVICE

	Tick, cross or blank*
■ Asks questions to understand customer needs	
■ Greets and interacts with customers in a friendly and enthusiastic fashion	
■ Adapts personal style and behaviour to match the personal style of each individual customer	
■ Looks for ways to help customers with their requests	
■ Exceeds, rather than merely meets, customers' expectations	

*Tick if behaviour was demonstrated; cross if opposite of behaviour was demonstrated; leave blank if neither

Summary of evidence:

____

____

____

____

____

Rating scale

Circle the rating that you give this candidate:

1	2	3	4	5
Weak performance, ie candidate displays 20 per cent or less of the behaviours	Some development needs, ie candidate displays only 30 to 40 per cent of behaviours	Moderate performance, ie candidate displays some 50 to 60 per cent of the behaviours	Strong performance, ie candidate displays most (80 per cent) of the listed behaviours	Exceptional performance, ie strong evidence that the candidate displayed all of the behaviours

Marking frame page 4 of 4

TEAMWORK

	Tick, cross or blank*
■ Observes colleagues and asks questions to see if other members of the team need help	
■ Puts forward own ideas and opinions as appropriate	
■ Prepared to back down and change own standpoint in the best interests of the team	
■ Takes on different roles as necessary to meet the team's overall goals	
■ Thanks others for their help and shares credit with others	
■ Brings appropriate people together to address problems that a single person cannot deal with	

*Tick if behaviour was demonstrated; cross if opposite of behaviour was demonstrated; leave blank if neither

Summary of evidence:

____

____

____

____

Rating scale

Circle the rating that you give this candidate:

1	2	3	4	5
Weak performance, ie candidate displays 20 per cent or less of the behaviours	Some development needs, ie candidate displays only 30 to 40 per cent of behaviours	Moderate performance, ie candidate displays some 50 to 60 per cent of the behaviours	Strong performance, ie candidate displays most (80 per cent) of the listed behaviours	Exceptional performance, ie strong evidence that the candidate displayed all of the behaviours

Sample completed marking frame page

The following is an example of what a single page might look like in a completed marking frame.

Marking frame page 2 of 4

DRIVE AND DETERMINATION

	Tick, cross or blank*
■ Prioritises tasks and activities	✔
■ Finds ways to deal with problems and barriers	✔
■ Goes the extra mile to get work done	✔
■ Asks for help from others when a work task is unclear	
■ Looks for ways to take on further responsibilities	✗

*Tick if behaviour was demonstrated; cross if opposite of behaviour was demonstrated; leave blank if neither

Summary of evidence:

Helen talked through an occasion when the computers crashed in the office. She was working on several client proposals at the same time but decided that one was particularly urgent and important. She tried to call the IT helpdesk but they were unable to sort out her computer problem. She went to another department to try to complete her project but also encountered the same problem there. In the end, she went to an internet café on the high street to finish typing up her proposal.

However, she mentioned later that there was another project in which she declined to help a colleague because (in her own words) 'it wasn't my responsibility'.

Rating scale

Circle the rating that you give this candidate:

1	2	3	4	5
Weak performance, ie candidate displays 20 per cent or less of the behaviours	Some development needs, ie candidate displays only 30 to 40 per cent of behaviours	Moderate performance, ie candidate displays some 50 to 60 per cent of the behaviours	Strong performance, ie candidate displays most (80 per cent) of the listed behaviours	Exceptional performance, ie strong evidence that the candidate displayed all of the behaviours

Deciding which candidate to hire

Once you have completed the marking frame for each candidate, you could write up the competency scores for all of your candidates and calculate their average or mean scores. However, making the decision as to whom to hire is rarely as simple as calculating a set of average scores and offering the job to whichever candidate gets the highest score.

Research shows that human beings are flawed decision makers. For example, we fall prey to both the 'primacy effect' and the 'recency effect', which means that we tend to remember the candidates we interviewed first and last; the candidates we interview in the middle tend to blur into each other and, left to our own flawed judgement, we're less likely to choose them. As such, following a rigorous decision-making process rather than making a snap judgement as to whom to hire will help you to select the strongest (rather than the best-remembered) candidate.

Setting a selection hurdle

A good start in trying to decide which candidate to hire is to plot the scores attained by all of the candidates onto a scoring grid (sometimes called a 'decision matrix'). Table 11.1 provides an example of a scoring grid for three candidates who were each scored on four competencies on a 6-point scale, where '1' represents 'significant development needs' and '6' represents 'significant strength'.

If we were simply to calculate their arithmetic averages (ie adding up all of the competency scores and dividing them by the number of competencies), we would get the average scores laid out in Table 11.2.

Based purely on these average scores, it would appear that Hilary is the strongest candidate and therefore should be offered the job. However, the candidate with the highest average score should not necessarily be the one who gets offered the job.

Table 11.1 Example scoring grid for three candidates

Candidate name	Hilary Ashmore	Larissa Petros	Alex Chung
Planning and organising	5	4	5
Teamworking	3	4	4
Communication skills	5	3	3
Learning and development	5	3	5

Table 11.2 Example scoring grid for three candidates

Candidate name	Hilary Ashmore	Larissa Petros	Alex Chung
Total score	18	14	17
Average score	4.5	3.5	4.3

Some organisations decide that certain competencies are more important than others and therefore put in place hurdles for certain competencies. The idea of a hurdle rate is to remove quickly from the discussion candidates who clearly do not meet the minimum requirements for the organisation.

For example, managers within this particular organisation may have decided *before the interview* that all candidates must score at least '2' or more on the competencies of 'communication skills' and 'learning and development' as well as at least a '4' score on 'planning and organising' and 'teamworking'.

If these hurdles had been put in place and agreed by managers within the organisation, then we can see from the scores in Table 11.1 that Hilary scored a '2' for 'teamworking' and therefore fails to pass the hurdle for that competency. Both Laura and Alex pass the hurdle, but Alex is the stronger candidate and therefore should be offered the job.

Examples of other hurdles could include: 'On our 7-point scale, successful candidates must score no less than a "2" on any competency as well as a "5" on "influencing skills".' 'On our 9-point scale, successful candidates must score at least "6" on "adaptability" and "leadership skills".'

However, bear in mind some of the following pointers when setting minimum score hurdles:

- Hurdles should be set *before interviews begin*. The danger of setting hurdles after the interview is that interviewers may try to set hurdles to get rid of candidates that they don't like.
- The hurdles must be linked to success in the role. The managers must be very certain that one or more competencies are much more important than the others in determining success on the job. Otherwise the hurdles risk being rather arbitrary – for example, managers could decide that they want only the very best candidates and end up setting hurdles that are so high that no candidates manage to pass.
- Hurdles should only be set by managers who are familiar with the role that needs filling. In the technical parlance, these managers are often called 'subject matter experts' (SMEs). The risk of having hurdles set by people within the organisation who do not have enough knowledge of the role is that the hurdles again become inappropriate.
- Candidates must clear each and every hurdle in order to progress. *Hurdles are minimum requirements* and, as such, failure to clear a hurdle on one competency cannot be compensated for by strong performance on another. Looking at the example in Table 11.2, the interviewers would not be allowed to argue that Hilary should be offered the job given her strong performance on 'other competencies'.
- If in doubt, it is better to set a slightly lower hurdle (or not to have one at all). The downside of discarding a genuinely good candidate because the hurdle rate has been set wrongly too high is greater than the potential time saving of having the hurdle in the first place.

It is also important to note that not all organisations set such hurdles. Many organisations simply calculate the arithmetic averages of the competency scores with the aim of hiring the candidate with the best score. Hurdles should only be put in place *for good reason and must be established before the interviews.*

Choosing 'all-round' versus 'spiky' candidates

Sometimes, interviewers may need to make a decision between candidates who have identical or very similar average scores, but very different profiles of scores.

Table 11.3 presents an example of a situation in which two candidates have the same average scores, but made up in completely different ways. In this organisation, candidates were rated on six competencies using a 6-point scale, where '1' represents 'significantly below par behaviour' and '6' is 'significantly above par behaviour'.

Figure 11.2 presents how the data would look if they were plotted on a graph. As you can see, Alan is more of an 'all-round' candidate in that he has neither notable strengths nor weaknesses. On the other hand, Tola is a 'spiky' candidate

Table 11.3 Comparison of competency scores for two candidates

Candidate name	Alan Lewis	Tola Adejumo
Thinking analytically	3	6
Planning and organising	4	1
Handling customers	4	5
Commercial awareness	5	2
Motivating and developing others	4	5
Technical knowledge	3	4
Average scores	3.8	3.8

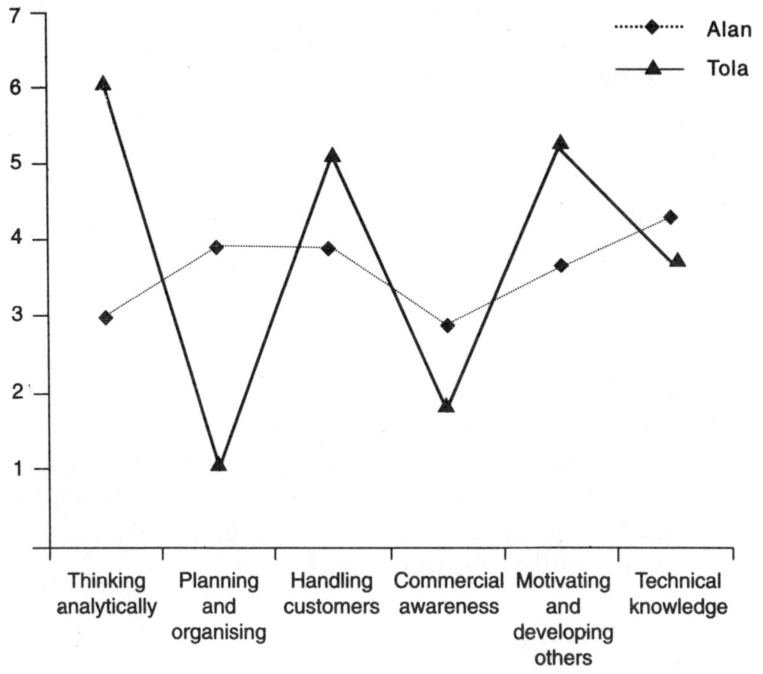

Figure 11.2 Graph of competency scores for two candidates

because she has both some key strengths (a '6' on 'thinking analytically' plus two '5' scores for 'handling customers' and 'motivating and developing others') as well as some clear weaknesses (eg a '1' score for 'planning and organising' and '2' for 'commercial awareness').

In this example, there were no organisational hurdles. Given that both candidates have identical overall scores, the interviewer must make a decision as to which profile of scores is more appropriate for the nature of the role. If the interviewer believes that 'thinking analytically' is the most important skill for this role, then Tola would be the preferred candidate. The interviewer may argue that it would be possible to compensate for her poor planning and organising skill by assigning her a personal assistant who could help her with her organising. On the other hand, if the interviewer believes that a lack of 'commercial awareness' was the main factor in causing the previous holder of the role to be fired from it, then it would make sense to offer the job to Alan rather than Tola.

There are neither right nor wrong answers in making such judgements. As an interviewer, you must make the decision that is most appropriate for your specific organisation and the nature of the particular role. However, to help you in making the right decision, consider questions such as:

- Which (if any) are more important competencies for the right candidate to have?
- If a candidate has weaknesses or development needs with respect to any of the competencies, how easily could you compensate for them (eg by training the individual, assigning other colleagues to assist the individual, changing the nature of the job, and so on)?

Bringing it all together

Table 11.4 provides an example of the scores achieved by four candidates, who were each interviewed against five competencies. In this example, the organisation has used a 7-point scale, where '1' represents 'unacceptable' behaviour and '7' equals 'outstanding' behaviour. In other words, higher scores are better.

In this organisation, the managers who set up the interview process have decided on an *overall* hurdle – that an average score of 4.0 is necessary for a candidate to be accepted into the organisation. In this case then, both Helen and Craig fail to clear the hurdle and therefore are immediately eliminated from consideration for the job. Only Narinder and Pete clear this hurdle. If none of the candidates had reached the 4.0 mark, the organisation would have had to reject all of the candidates.

Looking at the scores across the competencies, we can see that Narinder is the strongest candidate with an average score of 4.6. In an ideal world, Narinder would be the organisation's

Table 11.4 Example scoring grid for four candidates

Candidate name	Helen O'Davies	Pete Thompson	Narinder Ali	Craig Kimball
Communication skills	2	4	2	6
Attention to to detail	2	5	5	3
Customer service	3	2	4	2
Team work	6	7	5	2
Technical knowledge	3	4	7	4
Average score	3.2	4.4	4.6	3.4

first-choice candidate and the one who should be offered the job. With a score of 4.4, Pete is the second-strongest candidate – although only slightly weaker than Narinder (and still significantly stronger than either Craig or Helen). However, it is at this point that the interviewer may need to take into account other *factors* about the candidates such as their:

- knowledge of the job and their career aspirations;
- pay requirements;
- notice periods and/or availability.

For example, looking back at the interviewer's notes, it transpires that Narinder had only applied for the job because a friend had pointed it out to her and therefore she knew little about the organisation and did not seem particularly enthusiastic about taking on the challenges of the role. She also has a 4-month notice period.

In contrast, Pete had read about the vacancy and had done a lot of research into the role and seemed to be genuinely excited about the prospect of not only joining the organisation but taking on the challenges of the role. Also to his advantage, he had been made redundant several months ago and would therefore be available immediately. The interviewer therefore decides to offer the job to Pete. The interviewer decides that, should Pete refuse the job, the job would then be offered to Narinder as a second choice. If Narinder were also to turn the job down, the organisation would have to advertise the position again as neither Craig nor Helen was strong enough to take on the role.

As you can see from the example, the candidate with the highest average score is not necessarily the one who may end up with the job. However, at least by having the competency scores laid out in the above fashion, the interviewer can decide objectively who *should* be offered the job purely based on their skills. The discussion can then move onto other factors.

The overall decision of which candidate to hire therefore depends on two questions:

1. Does the candidate pass the competency hurdles (if there are any)?
2. Taking all other factors (eg motivations/aspirations of the candidate, salary requirements, notice periods) into consideration, which candidate is most desirable?

Table 11.5 compares three candidates who are being considered for a senior role to head up a new business venture. Each of the candidates was interviewed against six competencies and marked on a 5-point scale where '1' represents 'poor performance' and a '5' represents 'exceptional performance'.

Looking at the scores for the three candidates in Table 11.5 we can see that Carl and Tom are both equally strong with mean scores of 4.0 each. However, after some discussion, the interviewers decide that Carl's '2' score for the competency of 'leading others' is unacceptable. While both Carl and Tom have equal average scores, the interviewer decides that the challenges of the role mean that it is more important to have someone who scores highly on 'leading others' than to have high scores on 'strategic thinking' and 'driving change' (as Carl has).

The interviewer looks back through the interview notes taken on both Tom and Carl. Taking all of the other factors

Table 11.5 Example scoring grid for three senior candidates

Candidate name	Alison Jamieson	Carl Davies	Tom Fitzgerald
Strategic thinking	5	5	4
Leading others	4	2	5
Developing people	3	4	4
Working in a team	3	4	4
Winning new customers	3	5	4
Driving change	4	4	3
Average score	3.7	4.0	4.0

into consideration, the interviewer finds that Tom has a longer notice period and will therefore not be available as quickly as Carl. Tom is also more expensive – Tom earns approximately 20 per cent more than Carl. Even taking these factors into consideration though, the interviewer still decides that Tom should be the organisation's first choice. If Tom were to turn down the job, the interviewer decides that Carl's weakness in the competency of 'leading others' is too much of a liability for this particular role.

Finally, the interviewer looks at the scores for Alison and decides that there are insufficient strengths. If Tom does not accept the job offer, then neither Carl nor Alison would be offered the job and the organisation would have to try to recruit a new batch of candidates for interview.

Holding a wash-up discussion

As you can see from the hypothetical examples in the previous section, the decision as to which candidate should be offered the job is not always straightforward – and so far we have considered situations in which there was only one interviewer. If more than one interviewer has been involved in interviewing the candidates, you will need to invite all of the interviewers together to discuss the relative merits and demerits of all of the candidates to reach a selection decision. Such discussions are commonly known as 'wash-up' meetings. Depending on the number of interviewers involved, expect to spend at least 5 to 10 minutes discussing each candidate.

A process for wash-up meetings

When a number of interviewers come together to discuss candidates, it is important to have a process to guide the discussion in order to help the interviewers make the right decision in a time-efficient manner. Work through the following steps:

1. Begin the wash-up only *after* all interviewers have read through their notes and completed their marking frames, ie each interviewer has decided independently on the scores to give the candidates that he or she interviewed.
2. Plot the score achieved by all of the candidates on a table (see Table 11.6 for an example of the scores given by two interviewers, Judy and Chris, on four candidates, who were each rated on four competencies using a 5-point scale). For example, write the scores up on a flipchart pad or project them onto a screen so that all of the interviewers can see them.
3. Begin by looking at one candidate at a time. Seek agreement on the competency scores for each candidate before comparing the candidates against each other.
4. Look only at areas of discrepancy between the two interviewers. Looking at the example in Table 11.6, if the interviewers were to begin with the candidate Paul, they would not need to discuss the competencies of 'problem solving' or 'customer service' as the two interviewers both agreed on the same rating. The first competency they would need to discuss would be 'adaptability'.

5. Begin the discussion on any one competency by inviting the first interviewer who interviewed the candidate to summarise the evidence that was collected regarding that competency. In particular, this summary should focus on the behavioural indicators that the candidate did or did not achieve with regard to the competency.
6. Invite the second interviewer who interviewed the candidate to summarise any additional evidence.
7. The two interviewers should together discuss the evidence that they had collected between them to agree whether to round the score up or down. For example, with respect to Paul Grogan's scores of '3' and '4' on 'adaptability', the interviewers need to decide whether to raise the score to a '4' in the light of evidence that interviewer Chris puts forward or to lower the score to a '3' based on evidence that interviewer Judy puts forward.
8. The interviewers should then move on to the next competency for that candidate, finishing off one candidate and agreeing on overall scores for that candidate before moving on to the next candidate.

Table 11.6 Example table of interviewers' ratings of different candidates

Candidate name	Paul Grogan		Laura Tsoi		Jessica Hardy		Matt Abrams	
Interviewer	Judy	Chris	Judy	Chris	Judy	Chris	Judy	Chris
Problem solving	3	3	4	4	3	3	3	4
Customer service	4	4	5	5	2	1	5	5
Adaptability	3	4	2	4	1	1	3	4
Initiative	5	4	4	4	2	2	4	5

Keep in mind that the discussion between the interviewers should never get personal. Different interviewers are not 'right' or 'wrong'. Every time an interviewer makes a comment, it should be to introduce a new piece of evidence into the discussion about what a candidate did or did not do. Ratings for each competency can therefore be either upgraded or downgraded depending on whether the evidence is positive or negative.

To help make your wash-up discussions go as smoothly as possible, bear in mind the following pointers:

- **Allow adequate time for the wash-up discussion.** When there are three or four interviewers who have all met each candidate, it is not uncommon for the wash-up discussion to take half an hour or more per candidate. Trying to rush through the wash-up without adequately discussing the evidence for different competency ratings may lead to the wrong candidate being offered the job.
- **Beware of tiredness and boredom.** Interviewers can – and do – get tired and lose their concentration if there are many candidates to discuss. When a group of interviewers has been interviewing all day and decides to hold the wash-up session that same day, it is not uncommon for wash-up discussions to last long into the night. Make sure that there are breaks scheduled into the wash-up to allow interviewers to stay alert.
- **Beware of the 'halo effect' and the 'horns effect'.** Candidates often get rated on an overall positive or negative *impression* as opposed to competency-based evidence gathered during the interview (see also the section on 'Problems and errors' in Chapter 1). For example, avoid letting an interviewer claim that people from certain universities or business schools or organisations have all tended to be good or bad. Challenge such statements and make sure candidates are judged on the evidence that was collected *during* the interview as opposed to what was on their CV to begin with.

It often also helps to have present in the wash-up a person who can chair the discussion. The chair or facilitator should ideally be someone who had not interviewed any of the candidates. This person can therefore challenge the interviewers in an objective and neutral fashion and encourage them to stay focused on evidence rather than impressions. However, it is not always possible to have an independent chairperson, so it may be expedient to have one of the interviewers act as a chair as well.

The role of impressions and instincts

The purpose of a wash-up session is to discuss evidence against the competencies. Interviewers should be encouraged to bring up only *objective evidence* that they collected – and wrote down – during the interview. Interviewers should be discouraged from relying on gut instinct or general impressions alone.

However, that does not mean that instincts and gut feelings do not have roles to play in deciding which candidate should be offered the job. If an interviewer has a strong feeling about any candidates, the chairperson should invite that interviewer to explain why he or she feels that way. Other interviewers should then be invited to comment and offer up evidence to either corroborate or refute that point of view. If, for example, any interviewer makes statements such as 'I get the impression that...', other interviewers should be trained to challenge the statement by asking: 'What evidence did you collect during the interview for that?'

While we all have powerful feelings and instincts, the truth is that they are often coloured by our own, idiosyncratic past experiences and are far from infallible indicators of likely job performance. Feelings and instincts should be used to raise potential concerns. If there is no evidence to justify those concerns, then it is dangerous from a legal (and fairness) point of view to reject or appoint a candidate based merely on feelings.

Remember, in evaluating candidates, be sure to ask interviewers to back up their ratings with evidence from the notes taken during the interview. Do this by encouraging – or even challenging when necessary – interviewers to distinguish fact from opinion, feelings, suspicions, or instincts.

A worked example

Consider a hypothetical situation in which two interviewers (A and B) have each interviewed three candidates against four competencies each. In this organisation, candidates are rated on each competency on a 7-point scale, where '1' represents 'extremely poor performance' and '7' represents 'exceptional performance'. These scores are presented in Table 11.7.

As you can see from Table 11.7, there are a few competencies where the two interviewers have disagreed on scores. The first step is therefore to take each candidate in turn to agree on an overall score for each competency.

Table 11.7 Competency scores for three candidates by two interviewers

Candidate name	Kate Jeffries		Christina Kalinos		Douglas Barton	
Interviewer	A	B	A	B	A	B
Organisational skill	4	5	4	4	6	6
Team working	3	4	4	4	3	3
Commercial acumen	5	5	2	4	3	3
Interpersonal skill	4	4	3	3	3	3

Looking at Kate's scores, interviewer A has given her a '4' score for 'organisational skills' while interviewer B has given her a '5' score. Rather than simply taking the arithmetic average, the two interviewers need to discuss the evidence they collected in their individual interviews to decide whether to round Kate's score up to a '5' or down to a '4'. Their discussion goes as follows:

A: 'I gave Kate a "4" for "organisational skill" because she gave me an example in which she had planned a workshop involving colleagues from other offices up and down the country. In terms of behaviours, she broke a complex task into smaller tasks, calculated the time and resources she needed to achieve them, and succeeded in bringing everyone together. However, I did not hear evidence that she had created any contingency plans.'

B: 'Ah, I asked her to tell me about a project that she had organised that didn't go as she had originally planned it. I've got it here in my notes. She told me about a time when she had been responsible for organising decorators to come repaint the office reception area one weekend. The original decorators cancelled at short notice but she had been worried that they might drop out so she had sorted out a back-up, ie a contingency.'

A: 'OK. I hadn't heard that in my particular example, so I'm happy to agree on an overall score of a "5" then.'

B: 'Great, let's move on to the next competency.'

Looking again at Kate's scores, the two interviewers go through a similar process to agree on the score for team working.

By the end of the discussion, the two interviewers have agreed on the overall competency scores as set out in Table 11.8. As you can see, rather than simply taking the arithmetic mean of the scores (to give 4.5 for 'organisational skill' and 3.5 for 'teamworking'), the interviewers have agreed to round one score up and one score down in the light of the evidence that they raised during the wash-up discussion.

Table 11.8 Competency scores for Kate Jeffries

Interviewer	A	B	Overall score for each competency
Organisational skill	4	5	5
Team working	3	4	3
Commercial acumen	5	5	5
Interpersonal skill	4	4	4

The interviewers then move on to the next candidate, Christina. Looking back at Table 11.7, we can see that there is a significant discrepancy between the scores given by the two interviewers for Christina on 'commercial acumen'. Consider the following discussion between the two interviewers:

A: 'Budgeting is a big part of having commercial acumen. And I'm afraid Christina gave me only a small example in which she saved some money for the team by encouraging the people in the department to use the colour printer less and to use the cheaper black and white one instead. But she wasn't able to tell me how much she reckons the business has saved as a result of that.'

B: 'She gave me a much better example. She talked through a situation in which their office supply company was trying to charge her organisation more money. But she rang round several other suppliers to get quotes, put together a spreadsheet of the costs of using each of the different suppliers and then used it to negotiate with their original supplier. Let me check my notes... She managed to get a 6 per cent discount from the original supplier despite the fact they had in fact tried to bump up their charges.'

A: 'OK, I'm happy to go with a "4" score then.'

Again, rather than simply averaging the '2' score and the '4' score, interviewer A is happy to upgrade the score to a '4' in the light of evidence presented by interviewer B. As a result of that discussion, Christina's overall scores for each competency are presented in Table 11.9.

Table 11.9 Competency scores for Christina Kalinos

Interviewer	A	B	Overall score for each competency
Organisational skill	4	4	4
Team working	4	4	4
Commercial acumen	2	4	4
Interpersonal skill	3	3	3

Once the interviewers have agreed on overall scores for each competency for each candidate, they can then compare the candidates as they would normally do as if there had been only one interviewer.

Keeping candidates on file

You may occasionally find that you have a greater number of talented candidates than you have vacancies to fill. If you are lucky enough to find yourself in that situation, you may wish to consider them for other positions that are currently available, perhaps elsewhere within the organisation. Alternatively, keep their details on file so that you can approach them when similar opportunities come up in the future.

Deciding not to make any offers

Interviewing candidates should be about finding someone who will add value to your organisation – it should not simply be about hiring the 'best of a bad bunch'. Avoid simply making a job offer to the least unsatisfactory candidate.

Even if you are under considerable pressure from your colleagues to hire someone, you should consider the possibility of making no offers. If, for example, none of the candidates cleared the minimum hurdles that the interviewing team had put in place, you should have the confidence to explain this to your other colleagues.

Choosing not to hire someone may mean that the team has to work harder. But consider the downside of bringing on board the wrong person. A candidate who is too weak could make mistakes that cost the organisation time and money; a weak candidate could also put more of a strain on others within the team if they end up working harder to rectify his or her mistakes.

If you find that your colleagues challenge you over the decision not to make any job offers, be ready to defend your decision by citing the evidence for your decision. Refer your colleagues back to the person specification and the competency hurdles that had been agreed beforehand; explain the ways in which the candidates you interviewed did not meet your requirements.

You may then decide to re-advertise the position (perhaps in different publications to attract a hopefully better pool of candidates) and/or change the duties and responsibilities of the job so that you can look for a different (perhaps more junior or more senior) type of candidate.

Communicating your decision to candidates

One of the most commonly asked questions from candidates is: 'When will I hear about the job?' Candidates hate the uncertainty of not knowing one way or the other. Ideally, try to get in touch with all candidates – irrespective of whether they were successful or not – as soon after the end of the interview process as possible.

Communicating a 'yes' decision

Once you have decided to hire a candidate, you need to get in touch with the candidate as quickly as possible to share the good news. Remember that strong candidates often receive multiple offers from employers – possibly some organisations that may be your direct competitors.

Here are some basic pointers for getting in touch with the candidate you want to hire:

- Check your facts before you get in touch with the successful candidate. It would be foolish to make claims as to the details of the offer (eg salary, benefits, start date, etc) if any of those details have yet to be decided by, say, human resources. In particular, establish before you speak to the candidate how much room for negotiation you have on salary and benefits.
- Deliver the good news with a phone call first and then follow up with a letter stating the terms and conditions of the offer. If the candidate says yes verbally, be sure to seek confirmation in writing too.
- Make sure that the right person calls the candidate. For example, the person to call the candidate should have had a key part in the interview process rather than being, for example, a junior human resources person who had either little or no contact with the candidate.
- Do mention if the offer is contingent on the production of satisfactory references.

Communicating rejection

For every candidate you decide to hire, there will be a handful of candidates you decide to reject. Deciding *how* you communicate rejection to a candidate could have a profound effect on your organisation.

You want to retain the goodwill of rejected candidates. Rejected candidates who hear no news or who are treated rudely after the interview process are likely to complain about your organisation to perhaps dozens of their friends and contacts, possibly putting them off from applying for future vacancies within your organisation. Even worse, by not explaining your decision to candidates, you risk having candidates wonder whether you rejected them for some discriminatory reason. Most candidates find it easier to take rejection when they at least understand the reasons why.

To retain as much goodwill amongst rejected candidates as possible, consider the following guidelines:

- Phrase any rejection letters as positively as possible. Many organisations simply send out a standard rejection letter to candidates. If this is all you are willing to do, at least make sure it is phrased as positively as possible. However, bear in mind that rejection letters on their own come across as very cold and unfriendly.
- If giving feedback over the telephone, explain that you are not so much rejecting unsuitable candidates as picking the one(s) who were the strongest in the skills that you were looking for. It is usually easier to explain why the strongest candidate got the job than to dwell on what the rejected candidates failed to demonstrate.

Some candidates may push for quality feedback. They may ask about areas in which they could improve. If this is the case, consider the additional following points:

- Bear in mind that giving useful feedback enhances your organisation's reputation as a fair employer.
- Jot down some notes of what you plan to say. In this way you will avoid blurting out statements that could end up being misconstrued by a candidate.
- Run through what you intend to say to each candidate with your human resources and/or legal departments. Check that none of what you say could be construed as discriminatory.
- Explain that the decision was based only on the evidence of their skills and experience based on the answers that the candidate gave during the interview.
- Aim to give balanced feedback that focuses on both positives and negatives. Start by explaining the candidate's

relative strengths before giving feedback on the candidate's relative weaknesses.

- Be ready for counterarguments and some defensiveness. Many candidates try to argue about feedback. However, make it clear that all of the candidates were given the same opportunity to demonstrate their skills and that your comments are based purely on the evidence collected during the interview. You may need to emphasise that it is now too late to change your mind about the selection decision.

Checking references

Smart interviewers always make offers to candidates that are contingent on the production of satisfactory references. Surprisingly, many organisations fail to check references, which can be short-sighted as we know that a significant proportion of candidates falsify their qualifications, exaggerate their skills and embellish their achievements.

Interviewing is not a perfect science. There are some candidates who are so skilled at exaggerating or even telling outright lies about themselves and their experience that even the most seasoned interviewers cannot always spot them. Asking candidates to provide you with references provides you with one more way in which you can check that you really are offering a job to the right person.

Best practice dictates that you should obtain references in writing rather than over the telephone. The idea is that written references can constitute part of the formal record about a candidate.

However, response rates to written requests for references have been known to be as low as 35 per cent in some industries. So the ultimate decision as to whether to ask for references in writing or over the telephone is up to you. Perhaps the best approach would be to ask for references in writing, but if you do not receive a reply to pursue a telephone conversation instead.

Begin by deciding whom you wish to approach to obtain references about the candidate. Are you happy for the candidate to provide details of two or three people who can confirm his or her experience? Or would you rather gather references from specific individuals, eg the candidate's current or most recent boss?

I would urge to you be cautious about accepting written testimonials or references supplied by candidates (as opposed to being supplied directly from the referees to you). Candidates obviously want to show off their best sides, so will deliberately pick people to act as their referees whom they know will write positively about them!

Bear in mind that asking for a reference is essentially putting your faith in the judgement of a stranger, who may have his or her own agenda. *Best practice therefore dictates that you should only ask referees to confirm factual information about candidates* rather than to provide opinions about their performance.

In confirming factual information, the best person to approach is undoubtedly the candidate's current or most recent boss. Consider asking factual questions such as:

- 'Could you confirm for me this person's salary?'
- 'Could you confirm this person's job title and the nature of their responsibilities?'
- 'What was this person's absenteeism record like?'
- 'Were there any disciplinary issues that I should be aware of?'

Some interviewers believe that speaking – rather than writing – to referees may allow them to gather information 'off the record' that more closely approximates the unvarnished truth about candidates. Certainly, some referees are wary of committing in writing anything negative about candidates for fear of being sued.

Best practice suggests that you should *avoid* asking for opinions about the candidate's performance. You cannot know a referee's motives. For example, a referee who had a personality clash with or vendetta against the candidate could deliberately decide to scupper the candidate's career. For this reason, I strongly suggest that you avoid asking for opinions and instead trust your own judgement.

However, if you do wish to gather information about a candidate by telephone, consider speaking to at least two referees who are able to comment on the candidate's performance within the last year or so. In listening to the answers, watch out not only for *what* they say, but also *how* they say it. For example, a referee who hesitates considerably before giving answers may actually have concerns about the candidate's abilities. Think of further questions that you could ask to probe gently whether there might be any issues about the candidate.

If you uncover evidence that the candidate lied during the interview (eg about their salary, responsibilities, or some other fact about their job), you would have grounds to retract the job offer immediately. However, do remember that checking references is tantamount to taking the word of a complete stranger – you have no guarantees as to their impartiality or even competence. So be careful not to act rashly based purely on what a referee has said.

On the other hand, if the referees comment positively about the candidate, you should get in touch with the candidate to give him or her the good news: they've got the job!

A note on induction and development

Most organisations have some kind of induction programme introducing new employees to the working practices, policies, and culture of the team and wider organisation. There may be training in specific skills or techniques as part of the induction programme too.

The benefit of a competency-based approach to interviewing candidates is that you should by now have a good idea of the new employee's strengths and development needs. In an ideal world, the induction programme would include feedback from the interviewer on how the employee performed during the interview. The new employee and his or her line manager can then devise a plan for working together on the identified development needs (eg training or coaching) or find other ways for getting around them (eg reallocating responsibilities within the team). Given the wealth of information that will have been gleaned about a candidate by the end of the interview process, it would be a shame not to put it to good use in coaching the new employee and helping him or her to settle into the role more effectively.

12

Evaluating and improving the interview process

Evaluating the overall process

No matter how well your interview process worked, you should spend a little time evaluating how it could work even better. Try to gather all of the interviewers together as soon as possible after the end of the interview process to consider what could be improved.

Consider the extent to which you were satisfied with the number and calibre of candidates. In particular, consider these two questions:

- Was the *content* of the advertisement(s) appropriate? If there were too many unsuitable candidates applying for jobs, it may make sense to rewrite future advertisements to focus more on the downsides of the job so that only the most committed of candidates apply. On the other hand, if there were too few good candidates, it may be worth either rephrasing the advertisement to read more positively or changing actual aspects of the job so it becomes more attractive.

- Was the *placement* of the advertisement(s) appropriate? Consider the trade-offs between national versus local press, generalist versus specialist publications, advertising in press versus employing agencies or executive search firms, and so on.

Competencies

Consider the following questions with regard to the competencies:

- Were the competencies that were used to judge the candidates the *right* competencies? Should any competency be dropped or a new one added?
- Were the behaviours for each individual competency the right behaviours to be using? Should any of the existing behaviours be removed or rewritten? Should any new behaviours be added?
- If any hurdles were used, were these appropriate? As hurdles are a minimum requirement, consider in particular whether these hurdles were too high. It is less of a problem to have hurdles that are too low than to have hurdles that are too artificially high. However, if there were too many candidates passing the hurdles, should the hurdles be raised next time?

Number and structure of interviews

With regard to the number of rounds of the interview process and the number and length of interviews within each round, consider the following questions:

- Was the number of rounds of the interview process appropriate? Given that each round of an interview process should reduce the number of candidates by around 60 to 80 per cent, were there too many – or perhaps too few – rounds of interviews?

- Was it appropriate to involve the numbers of interviewers that were involved? Should there have been greater numbers of interviewers involved (eg the process took up too much of the existing interviewers' time)? Or should there have been fewer interviewers involved (eg to enhance consistency during the interview process)?
- Was the length of each interview appropriate? Was there sufficient time to probe the competencies in depth?

In answering these questions, consider also what feedback (if any) you may have received from candidates as to the length and duration of the interview process.

Interviewers

You may wish to ask the interviewers if they felt comfortable with their ability to probe for competency-based information. However, most interviewers overestimate their interviewing skills, so are likely to respond that they are more than happy with their own ability to interview!

However, it may still be worth investigating: 1) How confident do all of the interviewers feel about our ability to probe for competency-based information? 2) Should we consider bringing in an external consultant to observe and train us properly in the technique of competency-based interviewing?

If the interviews were conducted with several interviewers meeting one candidate at a time, there may be an opportunity for interviewers to offer constructive criticism to each other on their interviewing skills. If you do need to make any comments on a fellow interviewer, then consider doing it one-to-one in a private conversation as opposed to in front of other colleagues. Criticism is difficult enough to hear without having to worry about the added pressure of being criticised in front of others too.

Wash-up discussion

Consider the following questions to improve the effectiveness of future wash-up meetings:

- Was the discussion appropriately focused on the evidence that was collected against the competencies? A common problem in wash-up discussions is that the discussion focuses on gut feelings, instincts or impressions as opposed to the evidence that was collected during the interview.
- Was the timing of the wash-up discussion appropriate? For example, if the interviewers have spent many hours interviewing candidates, is it appropriate to have the wash-up meeting immediately after the interviews (which allows the interviewers to finish in only a single day but risks the interviewers being too tired to concentrate properly) or should the wash-up be on the next day?
- Given the length of the wash-up meeting, how much time do the interviewers realistically need to allow for future wash-up discussions?
- Should there be a chairperson/facilitator in future meetings? Or, if there was one and he or she was unable to control the discussion, should the interviewers decide on a new set of ground rules for the discussion?

Improving your own interviewing skills

In order to help yourself improve your interviewing skills, try to invite a colleague who is experienced in interviewing to observe you during an interview. Then ask for specific feedback about what you could have done better. In asking for feedback from a fellow interviewer/observer, consider working through the following questions:

- To what extent were my questions related to the competencies?
- Did I ask any questions that were less effective or inappropriate (see the section on 'Unacceptable and discriminatory questions' in Chapter 4)?
- To what extent did I probe to sufficient depth to understand the specific actions that the candidate took in each situation?
- To what extent did I demonstrate the 'active listening' technique (see 'Body language and voice' in Chapter 5)?
- To what extent did I come across as friendly and approachable?
- How well did I answer candidates' questions?
- How well did I manage the time during the interview?
- Overall, how well did I create a good impression of our organisation?

13

Creating useful interview documents

In helping yourself or other interviewers to make the best of the interview process, you may wish to create a number of documents for the interviewers to use, including a pre-interview checklist and an interviewer guide.

Pre-interview checklist

In the same way that pilots use pre-flight checklists to make sure they have not forgotten anything important, a pre-interview checklist can help you to make the most of the time that you have with candidates.

- Have you got a copy of candidates' CVs and covering letters and/or application forms?
- Have you read the job description and/or person specification for the role?
- Do you have the schedule/timing of interviews for the day?
- Do you know which room(s) you will be conducting the interview(s) in?

- Are the room(s) clean and tidy and free from distracting and/or confidential materials that should not be seen by candidates visiting your organisation?
- Have you put 'Do not disturb – interview in progress' sign(s) on the door(s) of the interview room(s)?
- Have you warned appropriate colleagues that you are interviewing and therefore should not be disturbed?
- Have you arranged the furniture in the interview room(s) to ensure that candidates will be as comfortable and relaxed as possible?
- Do you know how to raise or lower the room temperature (eg operating air conditioning and/or opening or closing windows) if necessary?
- Have you arranged to provide appropriate refreshments for the candidate?
- Do you have a notepad and pen for taking notes?
- Looking at the CV, are there any questions you need to ask about career history and/or aspirations (eg gaps, changes of career, etc)?
- Do you know which competencies you need to be interviewing against?
- Have you worked out the broad, open questions (as well as the follow-up interview funnel questions) that you will use to start off discussions about each competency?
- If interviewing with a colleague, have you together agreed on the questions you will each ask?
- Have you checked that none of your questions could be misconstrued as offensive and/or discriminatory?
- Are you ready to answer likely questions that the candidate may have for you?
- Do you understand next steps so that you can communicate them to the candidate at the end of the interview?

Interviewer guide

An interviewer guide is a more specific document that reminds interviewers of the information they should be aiming to gather. The more comprehensive you can make an interviewer guide, the more likely you will be to see the interviewers asking the right questions and collecting the right evidence. Interviewer guides can be a real help for novice interviewers who may be nervous about the prospect of interviewing; they are also particularly useful for helping line managers who do not interview frequently to interview in as consistent and effective a fashion as possible.

Different organisations vary their approaches to interviewer guides. Some organisations lay out in great detail the exact questions that should be asked; other organisations aim to remind interviewers of broad areas that should be covered or suggest questions rather than prescribe them. Whatever approach you decide to take, remember that while interviewer guides are useful in reminding interviewers of the key principles of good interviewing and ensuring some minimum level of consistency, they should not be used in a rigid fashion. Interviewers must be encouraged to ask thoughtful follow-up questions depending on the responses given by different candidates.

A structured interview can help us to make more accurate decisions about the people we choose to hire. This example guide provides structure and guidance for interviewing candidates applying for the role of Client Account Manager.

Example interviewer guide

Overview

The 1-hour interview has been divided into four parts:

1. Exploration of candidate's career background (*up to* 5 minutes).
2. Interview against three competencies (45 minutes):
   a Planning and organising
   b Serving customers
   c Working in a team.
3. Exploration of candidate's career aspirations and knowledge of the organisation and role (5 minutes).
4. Answering questions that the candidate may have about the role and/or organisation (5 minutes).

Further points

- Remember that the main purpose of the interview is to *collect evidence* against a set of competencies. During the interview, try to keep an open mind and simply write down what the candidate is telling you. Try to avoid judging the candidate or evaluating the information until *after* the interview.
- Aim to spend approximately 15 minutes on each competency. Give the candidate time to think about an appropriate competency; ask follow-up questions that *focus on the candidate's actions* and decisions, ie *what* the candidate considered and did.
- Be prepared to steer the candidate if he or she does not give you relevant evidence. For example, if the candidate spends too long talking about the background or context to the situation, you should interject politely and move the discussion on with an appropriate question.
- If you ask a question that does not elicit sufficient evidence, feel free to ask for an additional example. Bear in mind that evidence can potentially come from either their work or interests outside of their work.

Use the rest of this set of guidelines as a rough script to guide you during the interview.

Introduction

Remember to:

- introduce yourself by name and job title;
- explain that you will be asking questions about the candidate's career, their skills, and their aspirations;
- introduce the concept of competency-based interviewing (eg the need for the candidate to give specific examples of situations and that you may interject);
- say that you will be taking notes.

Career background

1. Please could you give me a brief summary of your career path over the last five years.

2. What do you consider to be your key achievements and turning points?
3. Tell me briefly about your current job and the responsibilities that you have.
4. (Add here any other questions on gaps in career history and/or changes of career if relevant.)

Competency: Planning and organising

Definition of planning and organising: 'Works out the series of actions and the resources needed to achieve goals that benefit the organisation.'

Opening question 1:	Tell me about a project or event that you planned and organised from the beginning.
Probing questions:	When did this happen? (If older than a year, ask the candidate to think of a more recent example – if possible) How did you start planning and organising it? What resources did you require to make it happen? What else did you do in creating the plan for the project? What feedback did you get about the success of the project?
Opening question 2:	Tell me about a project or event you planned that did not go according to plan.
Probing questions:	When did this situation take place? (If older than a year, ask the candidate to think of a more recent example – if possible) What was your original plan? What did not go according to the plan? How did you respond to that? What contingencies did you have in place? What would you do differently next time?

Competency: Serving customers

Definition of serving customers: 'Seeks to understand customer requirements and works to exceed them in order to win new customers as well as retain existing ones.'

Opening question 1: Describe a time when you identified an opportunity to improve the service you supply to a customer.

Probing questions: How long ago did this happen? (If older than a year, ask the candidate to think of a more recent example – if possible)
How did you realise this was an opportunity?
What information did you seek out in order to handle this opportunity?
What specific actions did you take to improve the service?
What impact did your action have on the customer?

Opening question 2: Tell me about a time when the team's relationship with a customer was under threat.

Probing questions: When did this incident take place? (If older than a year, ask the candidate to think of a more recent example – if possible)
What were the potential effects on the organisation of losing this customer?
How did this issue come to your notice?
What actions did you take to retain the customer?
What else did you do to retain the customer?
What was the outcome?
What did you learn from this?

Competency: Working in a team

Definition of working in a team: 'Works collaboratively with colleagues, providing support to both colleagues and external partners as necessary to ensure the achievement of team goals.'

Opening question 1: Tell me about a time when you made a significant contribution to a team goal.

Probing questions:
How long ago did this happen? (If older than a year, ask the candidate to think of a more recent example – if possible)
What was the team trying to achieve at the time?
What was your contribution?
Talk me through the specific actions you took that contributed to the team.
What impacts did your contribution have to the overall team?
What was the overall team outcome?

Opening question 2: Tell me about a time you were proud to have helped a colleague out.

Probing questions:
When did this happen? (If older than a year, ask the candidate to think of a more recent example – if possible)
What did you do or say to help your colleague?
What else did you do or say to help your colleague?
What impact did your assistance have on your colleague?
What feedback did you receive from your colleague?
What did you learn from the situation?

Career aspirations/knowledge of organisation and role

1. What do you like best about your current role?
2. What do you like least about your current role?
3. What do you hope to gain from taking this position within our organisation?
4. What do you believe would be your next career move?
5. Why do you want this role?
6. Why do you want to work for our organisation?

(Note: Questions 1 and 2 allow you to match the candidate's interests and dislikes to the vacancy at hand.)

Candidate's questions and wrap-up

Your final question should be to ask: Do you have any questions for me about the role or our organisation?

Finally, thank the candidate for their interest in your organisation and for taking the time to come in for an interview. Explain next steps, eg when the interviewers will be in a position to communicate their decisions to candidates.

A warning

An interviewer guide is an invaluable tool for interviewers. However, be careful not to use the same questions for too long. Candidates have many ways to get hold of interviewer guides – I have personally come across employees stealing copies of interviewer guides to help friends prepare for interviews. And, in the age of the internet, large organisations can easily find their interview questions posted all over job-hunting websites and blogs too.

The longer your organisation uses the same set of questions during interviews, the greater the risk you run of candidates learning of them and simply scripting 'perfect' answers. This is especially true if your organisation is a volume recruiter of many dozens or even hundreds of candidates for particular positions every year. So the lesson is this: Change your interview questions occasionally!

14

Final words

The quest for perfect prediction

The most fundamental principle of competency-based interviewing is that past behaviour is one of the best predictors of future performance. However, that does not mean that we can predict future performance with total certainty.

In the physical sciences, you can measure the chemical and physical properties of different materials; you can add one chemical to another and predict the result every time. Unfortunately, interviewing is not an exact science. Humans are too complex and you won't ever be able to get it right 100 per cent of the time.

Even the most seasoned interviewers will occasionally make the wrong decision. However, creating an interview structure that incorporates competency-based interviewing will help you to get it right much more often than you would do by relying on traditional, unstructured interviews.

Practice makes better

Introducing structured interviewing techniques to your organisation is an iterative process. The first time you and/or your colleagues use structured, competency-based interviewing techniques is likely to feel at least a little awkward. Some interviewers may even complain that they feel constrained by the questions they are supposed to ask. Other interviewers may forget to ask the right probing questions at all. But the second time the interviewers use the technique, it will feel easier. And it will become even more straightforward the third, fourth and fifth times.

When learning to use any new skill, it takes a little patience and practice to become skilled at it. So remind yourself and/or your fellow interviewers of that fact occasionally.

The two-way nature of the interview

Remember also that the interview is a two-way process. Competency-based interviews are not only more effective at predicting who can do the job; they are also preferred by candidates over traditional interviews too.

Candidates who are brought in for traditional, informal chats rarely say that they had a good opportunity to demonstrate their skills and experience. Candidates who attend well-executed competency-based interviews almost always say that they felt challenged and that the interview process was fair and rigorous. And that could be a vital difference when it comes to persuading your preferred candidate to join your organisation rather than your competitor.

Other methods of assessment

Some organisations use psychometric tests to gain further insight into the strengths and weaknesses of candidates. Broadly speaking, personality tests measure candidates' preferences – how they like to go about doing their work – rather than their ability. Aptitude tests measure abilities such as numerical and verbal reasoning or logical thinking skills. Before buying a test for use for your organisation, bear in mind that such tests must be administered by chartered psychologists of the British Psychological Society (BPS). There are many consultants who tout tests they have devised – but be extremely careful, as these frauds are qualified neither in their design nor in their deployment. These charlatans may even claim to have similar qualifications or to be members of equivalent organisations. But always ask whoever you are dealing with to prove that they are chartered members of the BPS.

Graphology, or the study of handwriting, is also sometimes used by employers in continental Europe to assess candidates. However, researchers have yet to prove that graphology can give any valid or reliable insight into candidates' likely performance. As such, be careful of employing a graphologist as you may risk being sued by rejected candidates for using an unproven technique.

Assessment centres are becoming increasingly popular. An assessment centre is not a place; it is a collection of exercises and tests designed to explore candidates' suitability for the job. The theory is that it is better to observe actual behaviour than merely ask candidates to talk about their behaviour – for example, it's better to get candidates to take a typing test than ask them to talk about their typing. In the same way, assessment centres try to get candidates to perform in job-related situations. At these events, candidates not only sit through interviews but also give presentations, complete in-tray tasks, engage in role-play exercises, and participate in group discussions. Assessment centres are an even better way to select great candidates than structured interviews. Once you have designed a structured, competency-based interviewing process and are happy that your interviewers are following it properly, you may wish to consider how to integrate assessment centre methods into your selection process too.

The 10 commandments

Here are 10 fundamental rules for getting the best out of your structured interviewing process:

1. Decide *well in advance of the interview* on the skills (competencies) that you want to test during the interview for the *particular* vacancy that you are trying to fill. You wouldn't use the same questions to hire a heart surgeon as for a rocket scientist, or even a customer service agent as for an IT manager. Find experts across the organisation who are familiar with the demands of the particular role to comment on the skills that successful candidates should possess (and therefore the behaviours that they should demonstrate).
2. Prepare by writing down a list of the broad, open questions that you wish to ask candidates. Ideally, prepare an interviewer guide that makes the interview 'idiot-proof' for even novice interviewers. Remember that you should spend around 70 to 80 per cent of your time during the interview asking competency-based questions.
3. Allow a minimum of 10 minutes during the interview to cover each competency – but ideally around 15 minutes per competency.
4. Ensure you ask questions about real instances and examples of past behaviour. Remember that the foundation of competency-based interviewing is that past behaviour is the single best predictor of future job success.
5. Probe in particular for detail about candidates' actions by asking plenty of questions *phrased in the past tense* to establish *exactly* what candidates did. If candidates speak in overly general or vague terms, challenge them.
6. Ask questions not only about candidates' successes but also situations in which they struggled or even failed in order to find out not only what candidates do well but also what they do not do so well.
7. Use the interview only to collect evidence – leave the

judgement and evaluation of the evidence until *after* the interview.

8. Take notes – avoid relying on memory!
9. Provide your fellow interviewers with a simple marking frame for rating candidates against a set of competencies in an 'idiot-proof' manner. Encourage them first to rate each candidate on all of the competencies before comparing different candidates against each other.
10. Encourage your fellow interviewers to make decisions based only on the *evidence* that was collected during the interview rather than on overall impressions, gut feel, or instinct.

Support for your organisation

Dr Rob Yeung is a psychologist and director at leadership consulting firm Talentspace. He specialises in working with organisations on selection and talent management projects. As such, he is often asked to:

- run workshops and speak at conferences all over the world on topics such as recruitment, selection, leadership development, and talent management;
- design competency frameworks;
- train managers in interview skills;
- interview candidates and use psychometric tests on behalf of client organisations;
- design assessment centres for selecting candidates;
- coach leaders and entrepreneurs in how to become more effective and grow their businesses.

To find out more, please:

- visit www.talentspace.co.uk
- e-mail office@talentspace.co.uk